WHY WAIT?
Create Your Soul Mate Now!

FRANK POLANCIC

Why Wait? Create Your Soul Mate Now!
JammyTime Publishing, LLC
Copyright © 2004 by Frank Polancic

JammyTime Publishing, LLC
P.O. Box 408017
Chicago, Illinois 60640-9998
Frank@CreateYourSoulMateNow.com

JammyTime, Six Degrees of Preparation, Soul Mate Census, Soul Mate Action Steps, Romantic Resume, Anti-Mate Resume, Soul Mate Resume and Alive Line are all service marks of JammyTime Publishing, LLC.

Publisher Cataloging-in-publication data

Polancic, Frank.

    Why wait? : create your soul mate now! / Frank Polancic. -- 1st U.S. ed. -- Chicago : JammyTime Publishing, c2004.

        p. ; cm.

    Includes bibliographical references and index.
    ISBN: 0-9753513-46

        1. Soul mates. 2. Mate selection. 3. Interpersonal relationships. I. Title.

HQ801 .P65 2004
646.7/7–dc22   CIP

Book design by Pamela Terry, Opus 1 Design, *www.opus1design.com*
Cover image created by Colleen Campbell at Campbell Designs
www.campbellartgallery.com
Cover image © 2004 by Frank Polancic
Author photo credit Brian McConkey@www.gratefulheads.com
Printed in United States of America

First U.S. Edition

WHY WAIT?
Create Your Soul Mate Now!

FRANK POLANCIC

JammyTime Publishing, LLC

This book is dedicated to my beautiful wife and soul mate, Thea Durfee Polancic.

Her love, compassion, wisdom, and partnership have inspired me to reach beyond who I know myself to be. Without her, this book would not have been possible.

Table of Contents

Acknowledgments

I'd like to acknowledge my beautiful wife, Thea. Thank you for editing this book and helping me fill in what was missing. I attempted to show you what you mean to me by writing it. Now the echo of the universe responds to you by others creating relationships like ours.

I'd like to thank God, Dad "Big Frank," my late mother Patricia, my brother John, and my sisters Lori and Teresa. Sean Gaughan, Matthew Ferry, Father Don Ours, Dory Willer, Rich Kelly, Laurence Keller, Marc Carpenter, Jenny Severson, Jen Krammer, Russ Schoen, Bob Adolfson and Mike Vanderwoude, Kraig Kujawa. Paul Gorney, Susan Griffith, Charles John Quarto, Diane Kuknyo, Claire Wexler. Joni Wheat, Janice Corley. Mark Drespling, Michael Losier, Lisa Maroski, Jill Perkins, Carlo and Colleen Cooper, The Ruske Family, The Capps family, Mike Morawski, Tom Murphy, Bergen Anderson, Mick Leavitt, Mike Ferry, Joe Mendoza, Pamela Terry, Brian Tracy and Paul Hartunian.

Special thanks to the following:

Mark Victor Hansen and Robert G. Allen whose book "The One Minute Millionaire" served as the inspiration for this project. The Enlightened Millionaire™ Commitment served as the model for my Soul Mate Declaration^{SM}.

Some of the concepts in this book come from Esther and Jerry Hicks of Abraham-Hicks Publications. I thank them for sharing their knowledge of the Law of Attraction.

All of the participants in my workshops. To the Chicago Second City Training Center for providing a playground for artists to hone their craft. To Landmark Education Corporation for making transformation and possibility available to everyone in the world. To all of my feng shui teachers. To the Neural Emotional Technique (NET) – a muscle testing healing techinque.

There are so many other people I would like to acknowledge. If anyone is missed I'll take care of that in the next edition.

Introduction

Are you ready to attract your soul mate? Do you fear it's not possible? Are you considering giving up? Are you still attracting the wrong ones for you? Are you with someone now and not sure if he or she is your soul mate?

Your intuition tells you that the right person is out there for you. What if you didn't have to look anywhere to find that person? What if it was as simple as completing some exercises that have nothing to do with searching? What if you just worked on yourself and then your soul mate miraculously appeared?

Dating is difficult today. Men and women's roles have changed. People's values have changed. We're impatient for immediate gratification. We want it now. And where do we try to meet people? Bars, the Internet, speed dating ...all while staring down the barrel of a 50 percent divorce rate. To top things off, the relationship skills we learned from our friends, siblings, parents, and the popular media are often inadequate and only serve to exacerbate the situation. With this kind of pressure, it's amazing that anyone succeeds at all!

Without the tools to break through these problems, we give up. As a result, we end up in a self-imposed prison—"the intellect prison," as Deepak Chopra calls it.

Find out what's keeping you from your soul mate. Learn how to create and attract your soul mate by accessing your own natural ability to have a happy, fulfilling, and loving relationship. Expand personally to discover your authentic self so you can explore your life's purpose with your new partner. Spend your time creating your soul mate instead of looking for him or her somewhere "out there."

I wrote *Why Wait? Create Your Soul Mate Now!* because I found my soul mate. Before this happened, I took specific steps and noticed that they brought her closer to me. I cracked the unconscious code to attract my soul mate. Whenever I started telling my story of how I found my wife, Thea, people gathered around to hear how I did it. Passionate about it, I kept a journal of the how-to's and aha's. Thea encouraged me to create a seminar to share my method with others. Many graduates of the seminar have found or are in the process of finding their soul mate at an accelerated pace. That seminar evolved into this book—a new millennium paradigm for attracting soul mates.

Most of us don't realize that we are all creators. Each day, each minute, we create thoughts, emotions, mindsets, and relationships. Each chapter of this book examines what you've created throughout your life, shows how you are responsible for creating it, and takes away that which you don't like. It's kind of like erasing your past. Then you'll start from a clean slate, where the possibilities of creating anyone you want are wide open. Through action steps, quotes, affirmations, tips, stories, and practice you'll gain facility with each technique to make sure you have a clear understanding of what to do.

You've been waiting too long to share your life with the ideal person. It's time to create your soul mate now!

Chapter 1

Open Your Eyes...Open Your Heart

"The person who tries to live alone will not succeed as a human being. His heart withers if it does not answer another heart. His mind shrinks away if he hears only the echoes of his own thoughts and finds no other inspiration."

— *Pearl S. Buck*

You may have heard about soul mates for years and never paid attention. Perhaps you already have an understanding and want to know more, or you just know you want to find that person and wonder if it's possible.

Let's start with first things first, namely, what is a soul mate? Before you can know what a soul mate is you must first understand what the soul is. In this chapter, you'll discover the many facets of the soul and what the term soul mate means to you.

What Is the Soul?

People have different ideas about what the soul is, shaped mainly by their cultural and religious beliefs. Here are some variants that will serve as the basis for our work together:

- Your inner self, as opposed to your physical self

- Immortal: The piece of you that never dies but rather lives on after physical death in another dimension

- An intangible quality that is impossible to describe

- The perfect self

- The heart, or your heart

- Infinite energy, never disappearing or dissipating, only changing form

- Your aura, the invisible "breath" or energy field surrounding you

Webster's dictionary defines the soul as "the immaterial essence or substance, the animating principle or actuating cause of life."

These are just some of the definitions of *soul*. In this book I refer to the soul as the higher self, that part of you that is all-accepting, compassionate, loving, and that thinks for the highest good of all people. The higher self comes from a place that keeps you ultimately moving toward a positive, happy future. Your lower self, on the other hand, thinks of pettiness, jealousy, fear, and anger, which binds you to negativity and keeps you anchored in the past.

It is important to reflect on the soul's importance in your quest for a soul mate. You're not just looking for a date or a good time. You're looking for someone with whom to share the divine part of your being (as well as the physical part). *Your divine being.* Let that sink in. You are creating a relationship that goes beyond "chemistry." You are creating a relationship that will be based in the expression of the highest self in both of you. Things like that don't happen by chance. They happen by synchronicity.

What Is a Mate?

Some think of a mate as a good friend or companion, a significant other, or Mr. or Mrs. Right. One idea to consider is that a mate is simply a person who is willing to join up with another person by conscious choice.

What Is a Soul Mate?

Soul mates are people willing to join with each other by conscious choice and from the definition of the soul, always acting from the heart and for the highest good of each other. Couples who are soul mates unite as equals in marriage and help each other carry out their highest path together. Soul mates move toward the good and betterment of humankind by sharing their happiness, fulfillment, and partnership for a lifetime.

The New Millennium Couple Meets! Bam! Wow! Pow!

While traveling around Europe, Laura stumbled upon the tiny village of Eze, France. One evening, she met several Americans who were preparing to go out for dinner, all of whom were staying at her hotel. A handsome man walked over to the group. "I'm Hans. I'm from Holland. May I join you? You look like you are having a lot of fun." Enamored by Hans's charm and conversation throughout the evening, Laura went back to Hans's room that night, and they made love. They spoke their passionate love for each other. "I never met anyone like you before, you're everything I asked for," Laura cooed. "Your beautiful eyes, your luscious mouth, our conversation. I'm so lucky to have found you," Hans romanced.

In all this bliss the two decided to travel together for the rest of their vacation. After spending one month together, Hans began to have second thoughts. He told Laura, "I'm not ready for such a big commitment, and this has all happened too fast. I'm heading home to figure out what I'm going to do with my life." "Hans, I can let you go, but what about all that we've built together in such a short time? We've had so much fun and laughter. I love you." Hans turned away, picked up his luggage, and walked toward the train. Was this Laura's soul mate?

Was Laura Hans's soul mate and he blew it? Were they on the right path toward "soul-mate-dom?"

Where Do Soul Mates Come From?

Do you find yourself wondering: Will my soul mate ever notice me? Will I notice my soul mate when I'm "supposed to?" What if he or she already passed me by? What if I was with that person and didn't even know it? Do I have only one soul mate and that's it? Am I dating him now? Am I married to her? Divorced from him? Do I even deserve it? I've been looking for so long—is it too late for me? Is it all just a matter of luck? One day I'm walking along and the next I'm in love and living happily ever after? Will my soul mate find me? Is it all up to God, Allah, Buddha, other gods, the Universe, or higher powers?

If you have asked yourself even one of these questions, now is the time to check your cynicism at the door. Know that you can have whatever you want. Be patient and allow it. You can search the world over—London, Hong Kong, or Paris, in nightclubs, churches, department stores, or on the Internet. In actuality, your soul mate can come from anywhere. You might meet your soul mate at work, in the dentist's office, at a party, on a blind date, or literally run into him or her on the street.

Open your eyes…. Open your heart…. Begin by opening your eyes wherever you go—and open your heart to the people around you.

You're a Powerful Creator!

At every moment you're creating your reality. Every moment of your life is a constant creation, the manifestation of your conscious and unconscious intentions, desires, fears, and focus. Moment by moment, we constantly choose how we want the world to occur and attract the people, circumstances, and things that will fulfill our idea of it. You created this very book in your life because you had the desire to find your soul mate, no? There are no accidents! In this way, every boyfriend or girlfriend you've had up to this point, you've "created."

What's our biggest problem? We don't align our conscious and unconscious minds, unbeknownst to us. Why do you think this is so? Because we base our choices on the past and what we are comfortable with, or from what we don't want but are still focusing on. This is why so many people marry someone like one of their parents.

So what's going to be different this time?

This time you'll have the opportunity to step outside that pattern, clean up your past, and create your future from a blank slate—from what you truly want, rather than what you're afraid is the best you can get. It's like wanting a Rolls Royce but settling for a Chevy.

You've identified what a soul mate means to you. Now it's time to see how you are going to manifest yours. Are you ready to look behind the curtain and see how it's done? Good! Let's get started with the fun stuff. In the next chapter, we'll look at how your own commitment will determine when your soul mate shows up.

Chapter 2

Measuring Your Progress

I'm sure you're ready to jump right in. However, before you build a house, you must create the foundation. This chapter lays the groundwork for your soul mate project. Following are structures that will support you along the way.

Declaring Your Commitment

> *"The dedicated life is the life worth living. You must give with your whole heart."* — *Anne Dillard*

Regardless of your current circumstances, the first step in creating your soul mate is to commit to your success. You have the desire; otherwise you would not have picked up this book. Now have the faith. Put your money where your heart is.

Soul Mate Action Step 1: Choose to be with your soul mate by signing your soul mate declaration^{SM} below:

> I hereby declare that I am committed to creating my soul mate with every fiber of my being. I give myself fully to the action steps in this book, and I trust that the work I do will allow my soul mate to come to me. The people, circumstances, and events are lining up in the Universe to support me in my journey. I will enjoy sharing my life with the one I love.

Sign _____ Date 8/30/08

To further demonstrate your commitment, go to *www.CreateYou rSoulMateNow.com* and make your declaration to the Universe. Or write me at *Why Wait? Create Your Soul Mate Now!* P.O. Box 408017, Chicago, Il 60640 and share with me your commitment.

Set an Alive Line^{SM}

The second thing to do is to set an Alive Line. What's an Alive Line? It is the opposite of a deadline. A deadline tells you when a project is over, when it's done. Nobody likes deadlines, whether at work, home, or play. The word *deadline* connotes finality, an ending, and dire consequences if it's not met.

An Alive Line is about beginnings, possibility, and freedom. It tells you when your new life with your Soul Mate begins. It's a "by when"—the date you set for your soul mate to appear. It can be six months, or it can be three months, or it can be a year. It's exciting that *you* get to choose your Alive Line, whatever feels right for you. When will it be?

You might be thinking, "That's ridiculous! This is a soul mate we're talking about. How can I just pick a date when there's so much I don't have control over?" Remember Goethe's wonderful words,

> "Until one is committed there is hesitancy, the chance to draw back, always ineffectiveness. Concerning all acts of initiative and creation, there is an elementary truth the ignorance of which kills countless ideas and splendid plans: that the moment one definitely commits one's self then providence moves, too.

> "All sorts of things occur to help one that would never otherwise have occurred. A whole stream of events issues from the decision, raising in one's favor all manner of unforeseen incidents, meetings and material assistance, which no man could have dreamed would have come his way.

> "Are you in earnest? Seek this very minute, whatever you can do, or dream you can; begin it. Boldness has ge-

nius, power and magic in it. Only engage and the mind grows headed; begin and the task will be completed."

The Alive Line is a contract with yourself and your soul-mate-to-be. You may not know who it is at this point, but the Universe does. With the skills you develop here, you'll be able to create the space and opportunity for that person to enter your life. Your Alive Line will motivate you to do extraordinary things, and the closer you get to the date you picked, the more "providence will move" to support you. You'll feel alive and vital.

What Alive Line feels good for you right now?

Soul Mate Action Step 2: Choose your personal Alive Line.

I am going to begin my new life with my soul mate by

Oct 1 Date _2008_

You can declare your intention at the website as well. Don't hold back. Let the Universe know!

Benevolent Pressure Is Good

Now you might be saying to yourself, "Well, that just puts me under pressure." It may and it may not. And if it does, pressure can make a lot of wonderful things happen. Remember that *you* get to set the Alive Line—no one is holding a gun to your head. Pressure is positive too; it keeps us performing at our highest level, creates emotion, and keeps us in motion. Some of life's most treasured work is done under pressure. Think of diamonds coming from coal.

Soul Mate Action Step 3: Plan and arrange to take a vacation either slightly before or after your Alive Line. Why? When you do something for yourself it raises your energy. With your energy raised, you are more likely to have your true qualities shining through, making you "attractive" emotionally, physically, and universally. And if you meet your soul mate before your vacation, you'll have something fun to do together.

My Soul Mate

A little later on, I'll tell you the story of how I met my soul mate, Thea, but here's a sneak preview. When I was down to the last two weeks before my Alive Line and I hadn't yet met my soul mate, I decided to step out of my usual routine and go to Miami for a two-day vacation. Getting outside of my day-to-day environment helped bring clarity and focus. Standing in front of the ocean at the water's edge, I asked God for my soul mate. Days later, on the day before my Alive Line, Thea came to me. She was exactly the person I'd asked for. I was even more astounded when I found out that "Thea" meant "goddess" in Greek. There's real power in Alive Lines.

Soul Mate Found in Two Months

"I took your seminar in September and set my Alive Line to find my soul mate by the end of November. I felt that was a pretty aggressive timetable, but I had faith that it would happen. I started to date someone casually, but he really wasn't right for me. I decided that I wasn't committed to just having a physical relationship without all the other things, and I ended the relationship.

A few weeks later, I was reintroduced to Jim, a man I had met about a month earlier through a friend when I was dating the other guy. I had thought that Jim was attractive when I met him, but I hadn't really paid much attention to him because I was seeing someone else.

When Jim and I met again at a party on October 24, through a series of events we spent the whole night together and stayed up just talking. From that day on we have spent all our time together and have fallen in love. I never dreamed that I could care about someone so much in such a short period of time. We both feel an overwhelming sense that our relationship was just meant to be and that destiny or fate has played a large part."

— Maureen

How to read this book: Give yourself fully to reading this book, like you would in your relationship with your future soul mate. Read the entire book at your own pace, and do not skip any chapters. Move ahead only when you're satisfied with the level or quality of work you've done. You might consider reading the whole book twice so you don't miss anything. Keep a pen, notepad, or journal nearby in order to complete the Soul Mate Action Steps^{SM}. It's a short book, so carry it with you and allow it to sink in. Your mind will have the opportunity to be at work while you are engaged in your daily routine.

CAUTION: The point is *not* to think about and intellectualize the material. Stay out of your head! It's about being in action and on the court, not the sidelines.

The Soul Mate Game^{SM}

Speaking of action, before we go any further I'd like to introduce a structure I've created to help you know where you're going and how to measure your success. As you do the work in this book you will be moving closer and closer to your destination—the appearance of your soul mate. However, while you are doing the work, it might not *seem* like you are getting anywhere, when in fact you really are. So to give you some perspective and gauge your progress, I created the Soul Mate Game.

How does it work? The game begins with declaring your commitment and ends with the appearance of your soul mate. Following are all the chapters from this point on:

Every chapter has specific Soul Mate Action Steps—exercises or activities for you to complete as you read the book. There are 28 of them in total—you just did three at the beginning of this chapter. At the end of each chapter, you'll be given the opportunity to reflect on how much energy and intention you put into these. Remember, the more you put into the process, the more you'll get out of it.

The magic occurs during and after taking the Soul Mate Action Steps, so do them. Don't rush through this book or skip steps. All the work is important to your success. Even minimal effort can produce big results. Any insight you have could bring your soul mate to you. Bring energy to the exercises, and results will naturally occur. You can guage your energy by circling your response to the Energy Meter section at the end of each chapter. If it helps you, use a partner or a team of people to hold you accountable. The more people you have supporting you in your quest, the better.

Affirmations

Each chapter also ends with a list of affirmations. Affirmations are powerful, positive belief statements that reinforce the mindset consistent with your success. There are many ways to work with affirmations. One way is to write the affirmation 20 times each day, each time noticing what your brain's response is to the statement. When your brain's response is "Okay, I buy that," then you're done with that affirmation. If you are an auditory learner, you may want to record yourself on a cassette tape saying the affirmation over and over, at different speeds and stressing different words each time. In addition to the affirmations provided at the end of each chapter, you'll find more affirmations on the website at *www.CreateYourSoulMateNow.com*.

I also recommend listening to the "Create Your Soul Mate Now!" affirmations compact disc. This disc contains dance music for each chapter with vocal affirmations that will encourage you to be alive, focused, and upbeat throughout your journey. You can find out how to get a copy of the disc on the website as well.

Soul Mate Census^{SM}

Before this book was written I had no idea how many soul mate couples there were out there in the Universe. By your declaring your soul mate status in the Soul Mate Census at the end of this book and at the website, I can begin to get a sense of it. Please go to the website and register when you have your soul mate. That counts as one soul mate couple. I am tracking soul mates that came about by reading this book and soul mates that were already together, so if you know of soul mate couples who are already together, please have them register and share their story too.

Soul mates are success stories! They enliven our hearts around the globe. They encourage and inspire us and light the flame of what's possible for couples. They are full of romance, magic, and hope. By sharing their stories, soul mates can help others fulfill their relationship destiny. By sharing the love you've found, you keep the possibility of love alive for everyone.

What made me think of this? Well, I was sitting around thinking about how wonderful it would be to track all the positive, long-lasting relationships. The good ones we hear about. In our society there are a lot of statistics about married couples, singles, and divorced people, but not soul mates. How can something so many of us are seeking not be accounted for? I am committed that as a result of this book there will be 75,000 new soul mate couples by March 1, 2006; 150,000 by March 1, 2007; 1,100,000 by March 2008; and 2,000,000 by March 1, 2009. Who knows? The number could reach as many as 30 million by 2024. After all, "You get what you focus on!"

Just picking up this book brings you closer than you've ever been before to identifying your soul mate. Attracting your soul mate is like a journey. Along the way, you'll leave the familiar behind, in the form of your old habits and thought patterns. You might also need breaks from time to time, as the work you'll be doing might be demanding or uncomfortable. Relax. Your soul mate is out there. When you've lost all faith, I'll believe for you.

In this chapter, you learned the importance of being committed. Next, you'll identify and let go of your old relationship model and create a new one that is aligned with your true desires. Are you ready for the adventure? Let's go!

Measuring Your Progress

1. I signed the soul mate declaration. (Yes)/ No

2. I chose my personal Alive Line. (Yes)/ No

3. I scheduled a vacation. (Yes)/ No

Energy Meter– (circle your response)

5. I did all of my Soul Mate Action Steps passionately and put more effort into this than I've ever put into a creative project. I'm elated, exhausted, and my heart feels good.

4. I did all of my Soul Mate Action Steps passionately and put in extra effort. I went beyond my comfort zone.

3. I did all of my Soul Mate Action Steps to my highest ability.

2. I did some of my Soul Mate Action Steps.

1. I read the chapter.

Soul Mate Affirmations

• I know that I can attract my soul mate.

• I am bold and powerful.

• I trust the Universe to provide whatever I need.

Chapter 3

Your Romantic Resume

What's a Romantic Resume^{SM}?

You probably already have a professional resume. It lists your education, your experience, your goals, your extra-curricular activities, and perhaps other things relevant in the working world. A Romantic Resume is similar. It lists your relationship education, your romantic relationship experience, your strengths, the good qualities you bring to a relationship, your hobbies, and what you most want people to know about you.

If you were applying for the role of being someone's soul mate today, what would your Romantic Resume say? (We'll get to your soul mate's resume later.) By this I mean how would you look on paper at this particular moment in time? What do you have to offer your soul mate? It's important to take stock of yourself first—to see what your strengths are and what skills and qualities you bring to a relationship. In doing so, you will come to appreciate yourself more and have greater confidence. After you have written your Romantic Resume, I'll guide you through a series of exercises to help you polish it so that it resonates at the highest and most authentic level of your being.

Here's a sample resume:

Name: Soul Mate Seeker
Address: 2650 Southport, Anywhere USA
Phone: 555-0023

My Personal Profile:
I am female, 25 years old, and have great communication skills. I am a loving, compassionate, and caring person looking forward to spending my life with someone who is open and honest like me. I have plenty of great relationship experience that will provide us with joy and happiness through good times and bad. I am strong and a natural leader.

Relationship Experience:
Lived with my loving family; mother and father, two brothers, and two sisters for 18 years

Lived with roommates or alone for the last five years

Have been loyal friends with Mary L, Rob K, and Jenny S

Always go to extended family gatherings monthly to keep in touch

I have really good guy friends. I love being a tomboy too.

My girlfriends and I have girls' night out twice a month. We all say what's on our mind, and that's what keeps us together.

Romantic Relationship Experience:
Everything up to high school is a blur. I kissed and held hands with eight boys.

My first true love was Jim. I went to high school dances with him as my best friend and dated him throughout high school.

I dated Pat for three years, took care of his needs, checked in, called, and was intimate and affectionate. I told him all of my secrets and vice versa.

I dated Terry for two years. I planned, organized, and created all of our dates. We always had something to do, and we didn't fight. We had great conversations about anything and everything. We took walks by the sea and kissed at sunset and sunrise. I loved it when Terry brought me flowers, bought dinner, and surprised me. Generous, polite, and happy, I always supported his goals.

I dated, for a short time, a few other guys and left them in good standing. We only dated a short time.

Relationship Education and Training:
Read *Men Are From Mars, Women Are From Venus* by John Gray

Read *7 Habits of Highly Effective People* by Steven Covey

Took a communication course at the University of Illinois

Participated in personal development seminar (e.g., Life Spring, Avatar, Tony Robbins, Landmark Education, Pathways, Spiritual Weekend Retreats)

Personal Skills:
I am adventurous and willing to take risks.

I am extremely funny and can make everyone laugh.

I am a great communicator and extremely well organized.

I am a budding creative artist; I write poems, screenplays, and songs.

I am highly intellectual.

I help at a homeless shelter twice a month.

Hobbies:
Competitive softball and tennis

Great scrabble player

Enjoy hiking, travel, and movies

I enjoy sports, chess, singing, and reading.

What I most want people to know about me:
I love helping and serving people.

I like fine dining and special events, like black-tie dinners and fundraisers.

Personal References Available Upon Request

Soul Mate Action Step 4: Of course, your resume will look completely different from this one, because you are unique. Perhaps you never dated anyone and were quiet and shy, or you really didn't need or want a romantic partner until now. Regardless of where you are in the process, this exercise is key to stretching your self-image in order to see where you are. Take 20–25 minutes to do your Romantic Resume.

My Personal Profile:

Relationship Experience:

Romantic Relationship Experience:

Relationship Education and Training:

Personal Skills:

Hobbies:

What I most want people to know about me:

Now that you have completed your Romantic Resume, take a minute to review it and reflect on what you wrote. What did you learn? What surprised you? Did you experience any embarrassment? Did you feel like you've done a lot or not enough? Did you notice any resistance to completing any particular part?

This resume is what we look like in a suit and tie, in front of people at our best. Sort of like the "Lights! Camera! Action!" in Hollywood. It's the spiffed-up version of who we think we are.

Soul Mate Action Step 5: Now look at yourself with no makeup, with messy hair, and wearing pajamas—what you look like when you wake up. A peek behind the scenes. This is your Anti-Mate Resume (see sample on the following page). Don't panic, it's only for a moment. On a separate sheet of paper, write down all the things you really want to hide about yourself, the things you're not particularly proud of. Tell the truth about yourself. What would your best friend (who knows the good and bad and likes you anyway) or your brother or sister say about you if he or she wrote your Romantic Resume?

Let it all hang out. You don't have to show anyone this resume (and I'm not recording this—ha ha), but it's important to acknowledge this part of you. Why should you do this? Because what we hide runs us!

Your Anti-Mate Resume:

Does yours look a little like this person's?

My Personal Profile:
I am a desperate 25-year-old woman who really wants to have children but fears that if I don't find someone soon, I'll be too old to have them and will have to live out the rest of my life in regret and victimhood.

Relationship Experience:
I'm not talking to three cousins and my sister.

Romantic Relationship Experience:
My last three relationships ended in fights.

I had two boyfriends at the same time once, and didn't tell them about each other.

Relationship Education and Training:
I learned how to be in committed relationships from my mom and dad, who have been divorced for 13 years. They taught me how to fight unfairly. My mom showed me how to cry whenever I don't get my way. My dad showed me how to withdraw intimacy when I'm angry.

Personal Skills:
I've been hurt, and I'll probably be hurt again, so I don't trust people completely.

I've got a temper, and little things set me off.

I can be righteous and stubborn.

Hobbies:
I have a lower golf handicap than all of my ex's.

What I most DON'T want people to know about me:
I am a loner and like my quiet withdrawal time—I shut down.

It should feel good to release these thoughts from your mind. Did you know that these negative self-images were lurking inside you? Were you afraid to put them on paper? Pat yourself on the back for doing this. This was not easy.

That's your past. It's not the truth about you (today or now). It's your limiting self. The energy you're putting into hiding this information is actually what gets you in trouble. Some of this may be the very reason your soul mate has been eluding you.

Later on, in Chapter 8, you're going to find out that "like attracts like." For now, in order for you to attract what you really want in your relationship, the first step is to acknowledge and take responsibility for this limiting side of yourself and then allow it to disappear. How do you do this? How can you release that negative energy from your being? That's what we're going to talk about next.

In this chapter, you've taken a close look at what you bring to the table in your relationships. You've got a lot of great qualities, and you want someone else to become aware of them and appreciate you. You have plenty to give. On the other hand, you've acknowledged that you're not perfect and have some work to do on yourself. Next, we'll get into the exercises that will allow you to release your limitations and negative energy and manifest your soul mate.

Measuring Your Progress

4. I completed my Soul Mate Resume. Yes / No

5. I completed my Anti-Mate Resume. Yes / No

Energy Meter – (circle your response)

5. I did all of my Soul Mate Action Steps passionately and put more effort into this than I've ever put into a creative project. I'm elated, exhausted, and my heart feels good.

4. I did all of my Soul Mate Action Steps passionately and put in extra effort. I went beyond my comfort zone.

3. I did all of my Soul Mate Action Steps to my highest ability.

2. I did some of my Soul Mate Action Steps.

1. I read the chapter.

Soul Mate Affirmations

- I am proud of who I am.
- Each action I take brings me closer to my soul mate.
- I am worth it.

Chapter 4

Clearing Your Environment

What's stopping you from creating the space in your heart for your soul mate? Your physical possessions! Odds are you have objects in your living space that remind you of past relationships, such as a picture of an old boyfriend or a wedding present, or even a college T-shirt. It may be something you don't notice or think about. It could be on your mantle or packed away in a box in the basement. These possessions could be awful reminders of a bad time in your life, or they could be beacons of hope and sources of inspiration.

In either case, take a deeper look at what these objects mean to you, why you still have them around, and whether it's time to let them go. In other words, we're going to do a little spring-cleaning in your physical and relationship space and make room for your soul mate to enter.

Clear Your Clutter

In Karen Kingston's simple yet powerful book *Clear Your Clutter With Feng Shui,* she says, "Clutter is stuck energy that has far-reaching effects physically, mentally, emotionally, and spiritually. The simple act of clearing clutter can transform your life by releasing negative emotions, generating energy, and allowing you to create space in your life for the things you want to achieve."

Everything in our living environment connects to someone, some event, or some moment in our lives. It can be good or bad, romantic or platonic, positive or negative. By bringing a new level of aware-ness to the subtle energies of our surroundings, we can often cause major shifts in our unconscious that go a long way toward achieving our dreams.

Soul Mate Action Step 6: Now it's your turn. Look at what you're hold-ing on to and get your blood flowing. On a piece of paper, write down all the objects in your space that remind you of a romantic relation-ship. Take five or ten minutes for each one and ask yourself these questions below.

1. What is the object?

2. Who does it remind me of?

3. How do I feel about that person now?

4. What does it mean to me?

5. What is the story attached to it?

6. What is it saying to me?

7. Why am I holding on to it?

EXAMPLE

1. What is the object?	Picture of Cathy
2. Who does it remind me of?	A steamy romance and lost love
3. How do I feel about that person now?	Lust
4. What does it mean to me?	She was so "hot."
5. What is the story attached to it?	We traveled around Europe; it was my first experience of freedom, so I cut loose and lived freely.
6. What is it saying to me?	I can't let go of it. I want more.
7. Why am I holding on to it?	I'm afraid I won't ever have such a great physical relation-ship again.

What did you find? Were you amazed? Surprised? Some of the items will feel relatively neutral. Others will have feelings associated with them so negative you'll want to throw them out the window and never see them again. Some you may decide to keep. The point is that all these items take up psychological space and potentially block your relationship energy.

You've Got Baggage!

An Old Flame, Extinguished

Amanda is single. Going through her closet one day, she found her old boyfriend Troy's football jersey from college. She realized she'd been holding on to it for the last ten years since they broke up. Why? She wasn't willing to let go of all the positive qualities it represented to her: stability, style, and toughness. When they were dating, she had thought Troy was "the one." But since then she had been in and out of relationships with men, all the while looking for those same qualities she'd found in Troy, and finding the other men lacking in comparison. As she held the jersey in her hands, she realized it meant she was waiting for someone like Troy. How could anyone live up to this?

Amanda decided to take a risk. She acknowledged and appreciated the good times she'd had with Troy—the laughter, fun, and trust—and then invited those qualities back into her life by setting the jersey free. She gave it away. A week later, Amanda found Eric. Eight months later she was engaged to her soul mate.

Soul Mate Action Step 7: Next, let's consider any objects from other relationships you have. These could be objects you've had since childhood or that represent something from the past. Did you get a second-place ribbon from the science fair and keep it to label yourself as someone who will "never finish first?" Do you still have a hand-me-down from your brother that is broken and needs to be repaired?

Your subconscious may be telling you "I have to take on other people's problems."

Expand your list to include any meaningful objects you find that fit into this category, answering the same questions for them. Take ten minutes to write down these items.

1. What is the object?
2. Who does it remind me of?
3. How do I feel about that person now?
4. What does it mean to me?
5. What is the story attached to it?
6. What is it saying to me?
7. Why am I holding on to it?

When you consider your living spaces, don't forget all the places where you keep your possessions, such as the attic, basement, and storage space, or even your parents' house if applicable. What did you notice?

Tip: Tucking items away in your attic or basement is the work of your subconscious. In your subconscious mind, you might be telling yourself, "I don't want to go there" or "I like it just the way it was."

Take the example of John. When he was seven years old, he received a red fire truck for Christmas. He loved it and played with it outside all morning. When it was time to go to grandma's house for dinner, John's father went outside to back the car out of the garage. Watching from inside, John was horrified to see his red fire truck behind the wheels of the family station wagon. He screamed and did everything he could to get his father's attention, but watched helplessly as his dad backed over the toy. His father's apologies were to no avail. He just wouldn't forgive him. Clutching the broken toy in his arms, he ran to his room. At that moment, he decided, "I'll never care that much about anything again. It hurts too much." Over the years, John could never seem to throw the broken toy away. It became a symbol of what happens when you care too much. Not surprisingly, when John was finally ready to fall in love, he had to let the fire truck go.

Like John, you too may find some surprises.

Three Magic Questions to Ask Yourself Before Letting Go!

Now that you have your list, it's time to determine what needs to go.

Q: *Does it give me positive energy?*

A: If yes, then keep it. When you appreciate the quality the item reminds you of, you will be in alignment with receiving that energy, thus bringing more of it toward you. The flipside is that you can also get rid of the object and invite a new but similar energy into your life. It starts with your specific intention. If it represents laughter, let go of the old laughter and intend to let new laughter begin. It can happen quickly. Strange coincidences or synchronicity will happen immediately.

Q: *Does it take away my energy?*

A: If yes, then get rid of it. Sell it, trade it, donate it, or give it away to someone who will see value in it. It might be easy to do, or there may be resistance. Be smart about it. If it's a diamond ring worth $25,000, don't throw it away. Sell it or give it to a loved one. Think about its negative energy and set the intention to release the grip that energy has on you. Ask the Universe to send you better things.

Q: *Will I move forward or stay stuck by having this object in my presence?*

A: If you're going to move forward, then keep it. If it truly represents who you are and where you're going, then enjoy it.

A: If you're going to stay stuck, then say adios, auf Wiedersehen, good-bye to that object.

Soul Mate Action Step 8: Go through your list and mark the items you've chosen to let go of. Also indicate the date by which you will let go. Schedule this in your calendar.

Remember, they are only material belongings. That's it. They can be replaced. It's not life or death. It's "Does this give me life or not?" The benefits of not having an object can outweigh the benefits of keeping it. You have the courage to release an object's grip on you. Stop procrastinating and start activating new energy.

Our parents' generations were not up-to-speed on the limiting effects clutter has on us. In fact, many people who lived through the rationing of World War II are still holding on to things, thinking that's the way they will avoid not having enough. They never want to experience the scarcity they lived through during the war. Our generation has unconsciously absorbed these same mentalities, and they continue to affect us.

It's extremely important to trust what you feel, your instincts, or what comes directly to your mind immediately when you pick up the object. From songs, presents, and wedding gifts to old love letters and photos—don't hesitate to let go. The bottom line is you've got a lot of stuff in your home, and if you want to create your soul mate, it is a good idea to analyze your possessions and take courageous action so you can move forward.

Don't be surpirsed if you experience "a ripple effect" in your community. Because you're getting rid of things, family, friends, coworkers, and ex's will be doing the same. It acknowledges how powerful you are and your positive effect on others. Do not take this lightly. People love and admire your being a leader and getting to your true self or core. Even though they may not do it at the same speed, they are transforming their lives in the process too.

Soul Mate Action Step 9: Come to terms with a possession that you really don't want to let go of. Now let go of it.

Quantum Leap and Inspiring Results

Jennifer had been dating Jack for four years when she finally let go. Jennifer, who had been married in the past, sold the wedding dress from her previous marriage. Less than a month later she and Jack were engaged. Coincidentally, her fiancé bought the ring during the very same week that Jennifer got rid of her dress. If it was to be, it was up to her.

Can you see how this is all linked?

My Three Favorite Most Commonly Overlooked Possessions

One - What's possibly your largest possession? If you're a homeowner, it's your house. If your home no longer delights and energizes you when you're there, then improve, repair, or expand it. If that doesn't excite you, then sell your home and move. Seem extreme? The impact your home has on you is enormous. It's the space where you rest, dream, and play. It's the space that defines you. You can't afford to have it de-energize you.

Two - Is your environment filled with things in need of repair? These items drain your energy. Repair or replace them.

Three - Pay particular attention to the music you own and what specific songs or albums mean to you. Songs store your emotions like a time capsule. When did you start listening to your favorite style of music? Probably when you were a teenager. Have you ever heard a song and had it immediately take you back to the time when you first heard it, or the person you were with? Subconsciously, songs will remind you of past times in your life—good or bad, romantic or platonic. Take time to go through your music collection and let go of songs or albums that make you sad, angry, or unhappy or that keep you rooted in a past relationship.

A Final Note: Do not go out and buy replacement objects just yet. Wait until you've read Chapters 8, 9, and 10. These chapters will help you focus on what to buy. Continue clearing your space until then.

Are you relieved, more energetic, magnetic, and feeling more attractive? Did someone show up in your life during this clutter-clearing period? Are you thinking that he or she might be your soul mate? Let's wait and see.

It feels good knowing what to do with that stuff, doesn't it? So far, you've learned that every part of your physical life, even your house, means something and can influence your relationships. You are clearly responsible for causing your relationships to move forward or not. You are becoming conscious of your environment. As you move forward, you'll be able to continue this process. If you have nothing in your environment, you're lucky, because in Chapter 10 you will learn to visualize and acquire the right items for creating your soul mate.

We just dealt with one kind of closure—that of your physical space or surroundings such as your home, your parents' house, or the place you work. The other closure occurs in your internal mental and emotional environment and in your communication with other people.

Are you still thinking about the people you can't seem to get closure on? You'll soon discover how to create even more closure by speaking directly to them. Get ready for a burst of momentum that's going to carry you into an exciting realm of creation. Are you ready?

Measuring Your Progress

6. I wrote down all romantic objects. Yes / No

7. I wrote down all of the platonic objects. Yes / No

8. I've chosen my items and the date I'll let go. Yes / No

9. I let go of an object I was not willing to let go of before. Yes / No

Energy Meter– (circle your response)

5. I did all of my Soul Mate Action Steps passionately and put more effort into this than I've ever put into a creative project. I'm elated, exhausted, and my heart feels good.

4. I did all of my Soul Mate Action Steps passionately and put in

extra effort. I went beyond my comfort zone.

3. I did all of my Soul Mate Action Steps to my highest ability.

2. I did some of my Soul Mate Action Steps.

1. I read the chapter.

Soul Mate Affirmations

• I am inspired to clear away the clutter in all areas of my life.

• I welcome change and new energy in my home.

• I trust my instincts.

Chapter 5

Appreciation and Closure

"Only the hand that erases can write the true thing."
— Meister Eckhart

Do you have fond memories of past relationships? Do you wonder how you can get those experiences back? Are you still thinking about the ones that got away? Or, on the other hand, are you feeling sad or angry about how some of your relationships ended? Are you still unwilling to forgive your ex's? Is it still unclear why the relationship ended? Were *you* left hanging?

In this chapter, we'll look at how you can make the most of your past relationships. You'll learn to acknowledge all the good relationships in your life so that you can bring more of them to you. You'll also learn how to bring closure to any past relationships that were left incomplete. This will leave you with a sense of power, peace, and fulfillment and a clear space for a wonderful new relationship to enter.

Past Romantic Relationships

As in the last chapter we'll work with both your romantic and platonic relationships.

Let's start with the romantic category. It's important to acknowledge and appreciate all the wonderful aspects of your past relationships and the people you dated. If we follow the rule that "you get what you focus on," creating a mindset of gratitude and appreciation will help attract more great experiences into your life. Suppose you were in a relationship with a handsome man who always brought you flowers, called you with surprises when you least expected it, and had conversations that were always extraordinary. You would definitely want to acknowledge that person for being so generous and, equally important, yourself for attracting such a great person into your life.

Soul Mate Action Step 10: Take five or ten minutes to think about the things you really liked about your past romantic relationships. Then, pick your top five most memorable relationships and write down all the attributes you liked about the person and the relationship. Use the following questions as a guide.

1. Who is it?

2. What do I appreciate about him or her?

3. How did that person make me feel?

4. What would I like to acknowledge him or her for?

5. What do I want most for him or her?

How do you feel now? Acknowledgment feels pretty good, doesn't it? As a bonus, have a conversation with each person on your list to acknowledge everything wonderful he or she was and did in your relationship. Sound risky? Good! I promise you the benefit will far outweigh any initial discomfort or shyness you might feel. In Chapter 8, you can revisit acknowledgment and the powerful role it plays in attracting the results you want in life.

Past Platonic Relationships

In Plato's dialogue *The Symposium*, three types of love are discussed: eros (romantic love), agape (the love between friends), and philia (like the love of good wine or music). Today, *platonic* refers to a type of love you have for someone else that is not romantic; it's another way of labeling what Plato called agape.

It's important to acknowledge and appreciate all the wonderful qualities of people with whom you've had platonic relationships too.

Perhaps you and your sister are like best friends to each other. Maybe you have an uncle who is always looking out for you. Or your brother always includes you in the fun things he does. Have you ever had a conversation with these people and told them how much you appreciate them?

How about your parents? God? When was the last time you thanked your father for providing food and shelter, or for just being your dad? If you're spiritual, when was the last time you really thanked God for the blessings in your life? We often say, "Actions speak louder than words," but sometimes taking the time to acknowledge someone is more meaningful to that person and an even greater act of generosity from you.

How about your relationship to yourself? We each have fantastic qualities that we rarely honor ourselves for, usually under the guise of being modest or humble. Now is not the time to be stingy! After all, you deserve the best of soul mates, don't you?

Soul Mate Action Step 11: Now is a great time to appreciate the people in your platonic relationships too. Take as much time as you need to list the people in your life you'd like to honor. Have at least three people on your list, including yourself. Use the questions from *Action Step 10* as a guide.

By the way, after doing these exercises you might notice an increase in coincidences or synchronistic events happening to you. For instance, you might find that while you're thinking about your father he suddenly calls. For fun, make a note of these occurrences on your list.

Soul Mate Action Step 12: Take 15 minutes and call or visit one of those people and let them know what you appreciate about them.

Why is it important to bring appreciation to your past relationships? First, it increases your awareness of what you enjoy most in your relationships. This awareness will be very useful in the work we do in Chapter 8, when you begin to define your ideal soul mate. Second, as I mentioned above, having your focus on the positive will draw more of that to you. Now let's look at the other side of the equation, closure.

Bringing Closure to Your Past Relationships

Equally as important as appreciating people is bringing closure to the relationships that are currently not working or did not work in the past. Closure means cleaning up or completing the incomplete parts of your past—for instance, saying all of the things that were left unsaid, or doing what you wish you would have done then.

How can you tell whether you do or don't have closure in a relationship? We've all been hurt before. We've also caused hurt to others. Some of us more than others. Some of us deeper than others. When you think about a past or present relationship, if you still feel hurt or guilty, you still don't have closure. Think of a relationship (romantic or platonic) you have now that isn't working or a past relationship that didn't work. Who is the first person that comes to mind? How do you feel when you think about him or her?

Why is closure important? If not released in some way, negative emotions pile up and linger, sometimes long past the lifetime of the relationship, like algae in a fishbowl. With your vision "clouded" by sadness, anger, frustration, or guilt, it's difficult to create a new relationship without being cynical or hesitant.

This isn't to say that creating closure is easy. On the contrary, it takes real courage! Unlike appreciation, creating closure with another person can be painful and embarrassing, and we humans—like any animal—instinctively avoid pain. However, beyond the risk is great reward. Going back and tying up the loose ends of "incomplete" relationships, regardless of how bad they were, sets you free.

It Was Over Long Before It Ended

I realize now that I had 'left' my relationship with Laura long before it ended. I knew it wasn't going to work, and I withdrew about six months into it. She went off and cheated on me around this time, and I blamed her for ruining the relationship. I felt totally justified.

Afterwards, when I told her how disappointed I was about her actions and took responsibility for my half not working, she seemed greatly relieved and pleased to hear

it. I felt much better and could move forward with a clear
conscience.   — Ted

Conclusion brings peace to any unsolved areas of your relationships
so you can start with a clean slate. It's like pouring the old stale coffee
out before getting a refill. You can't welcome something new into a
space that's already full! You must dig away the past to clear the space
for new and positive things to show up. This is critical for the work
we'll do later in creating your soul mate. Make sense? Now you can
bring some closure to your relationships.

Bringing Closure to Romantic Relationships

Soul Mate Action Step 13: Take five or ten minutes to think about your
romantic relationships. With whom do you feel some lingering guilt
or negativity? Answer the following questions.

1. Who is it?

2. What aspects of the relationship are or were unsatisfying?

3. What do I feel when I think about that person?

4. What patterns in that relationship keep reoccurring in my life?

How did that feel? Was it painful, sad, or freeing? All the feelings
you have are valid. The next step is to take the action required to
bring closure to these relationships. Have a conversation.

Which relationships are you willing to heal?

Before you get into dialogue with these people, it's essential that
you ask yourself the following question and be totally honest: What
role did **each** of us play in this? Naturally, we'll want to point the
finger at the other person. We humans are pretty self-righteous by
nature. However, as they say, "It takes two to tango." It might take
awhile, but sit with the question for as long as it takes to see what role
you played in the negative emotions you feel.

There may be some ugly things you won't want to admit to the
other person. Maybe he or she was asking for something you could
clearly give and you were too stubborn to give it (like just letting her

have her way for a change). It could be something not communicated; for example, you broke up with someone in your head but didn't tell the person, and just became unavailable or cold until he or she broke up with you. Usually the greater the emotional charge, the more likely there's a role you played in the matter.

Soul Mate Action Step 14a: First, look back at your list from *Action Step 13*. Is there anyone you need to add? If so, add that person's name to your list. For each person, answer the following additional questions.

1. Do I need to forgive him or her? If so, for what?

2. Do I need for that person to forgive me? If so, for what?

3. What can I take responsibility for?

4. What do I want most <u>from</u> him or her?

5. What do I want most <u>for</u> him or her?

Soul Mate Action Step 14b: Once you have answered the questions above and are clear about your role in the matter, choose whom you'll call first. Take a deep breath and pick up the phone.

In your conversation, make sure to say anything you need to be complete in the relationship. It probably won't be as scary as you think. In fact, expect to feel happy and relieved. Remember the prize—the soul mate who is coming to you. When you're ready, call the next person. The good news is that this list is not infinite, and most likely you'll have only a few "biggies."

CAUTION: The other person probably knows how to push your buttons. Before you call, take some deep breaths, and imagine yourself being able to stay calm and appreciative no matter what she or he says. Be prepared for anything—but focus on the best outcome!

How did that feel? Was it as scary as you thought it would be? However your conversations went, congratulate yourself on a job well done. Find some way to reward yourself or celebrate your new freedom.

No one said this would be easy, but the nice thing about closure is that once you're complete with the relationship or the issue between you and that other person, it most likely no longer comes up. If it does, then you may need to have another conversation, or simply let it go.

Come back to the exercises above as often as you need to. For some of those relationships, you may only need to communicate with one person about one issue, and that issue gets completed in other areas with other people too. It sends a ripple to your romantic relationship community and the people who surround you. Good news travels fast and shifts people's perceptions about you in a wonderful new way. I know at some level your soul mate is listening too.

Bringing Closure to Platonic Relationships

> *"Love is an act of endless forgiveness, a tender look which becomes a habit."*   *— Peter Ustinov*

Now that you have some experience, let's move on to your platonic relationships. Even in present, continuing relationships, it's important to bring closure to any past events about which you still feel some lingering negativity. Not only for the purpose of creating your soul mate, but also for the health of the relationship, it's important to clear the decks occasionally with the ones you love.

Soul Mate Action Step 15: Think of any relationships with family or close friends that aren't working as well as you'd like them to. You may include yourself or God too. Repeat *Action Steps 13*, *14a* and *14b* for each of these people as well.

What do I do about the people I can't find or who have passed away?

Do whatever it takes to find the other person. Call Directory Assistance to get his new phone number. Use www.peoplesearch.com. The Internet makes finding people very easy. Go online to search for her new address. Visit her gravesite. Ask a friend or relative where he is living now.

When you can't get in touch with someone on your list for whatever reason, it's best to write a letter and send it out to the Universe. If you want to, mail it to where you think the person is and don't include a return address. If you weren't able to attend the funeral of someone on your list, attend someone else's—as odd as that may sound. It could be a powerful way to experience the person's passing and to say what you need to say to be complete. The important thing is to do something, and magically the Universe will respond. You may even experience one of those synchronistic events in the form of an unexpected phone call, e-mail, or letter.

In this chapter, you've done considerable work! You've learned to appreciate the people in your life and to bring closure to relationships. You've worked with both the romantic and platonic relationships in your life. This was probably the toughest part of the work you'll do in creating your soul mate, and I promise you it will pay off. Before you can create anything new, you must have a clean space in which to create, free from the limitations of your past. That's what you've just done. Great work. Next you'll look at your current dating behaviors and patterns.

Measuring Your Progress

10. I appreciated my romantic relationships. Yes / No

11. I appreciated my platonic relationships. Yes / No

12. I acknowledged selected people "live." Yes / No

13. I created my closure list for romantic relationships. Yes / No

14a. I added to my list and answered the questions. Yes / No

14b. I communicated with all or some of those people. Yes / No

15. I created my closure list for platonic. Yes / No
I added to my list and answered the questions. Yes / No
I communicated with all of those people. Yes / No

Energy Meter– (circle your response)

5. I did all of my Soul Mate Action Steps passionately and put more effort into this than I've ever put into a creative project. I'm elated, exhausted, and my heart feels good.

4. I did all of my Soul Mate Action Steps passionately and put in extra effort. I went beyond my comfort zone.

3. I did all of my Soul Mate Action Steps to my highest ability.

2. I did some of my Soul Mate Action Steps.

1. I read the chapter.

Soul Mate Affirmations

- I love to appreciate people.
- My thoughts and actions honor everyone around me.
- I am 100% responsible for my relationships.

Chapter 6

Successful Dating

A re you tired of the same old dating routine? Do you seem to be stuck in a dating rut? Do dating games bore you? Do you find that you're not sure where you stand after you've dated awhile? Since you're reading this book, I'd guess your answer to at least one of these questions is "yes."

In this chapter, you'll identify the dating habits that limit you and keep you from creating your soul mate. You'll create new habits that are appropriate for the person you are today and replace ineffective strategies you may have created throughout your dating history.

What Are Dating Habits?

Like any other habits, dating habits are patterns or rules of behavior that you repeat and that are consistent and normal for you. Amazingly, most of these dating habits come from our first experiences of "falling in love" on the playground and in the halls of elementary school, as well as from what we learned from family, friends, TV, and magazines.

In our first romantic encounters, we created rules of engagement, often based in shyness and fear—fear both of the object of our affection and the opinions of our peers. Some examples of these rules are:

The man should always ask the woman out.

The woman should be a good listener and let the man talk.

Never kiss a woman on the first date—she'll respect you for that.

You should get to "first base" on the first date, "second base" next, and so on.

No kidding! Who said this was true? Now we are adults, still employing the same strategies. As adults, these early decisions lurk beneath the surface and unconsciously continue to guide our decisions and behavior with those people we're interested in. The scary thing is that these habits determine your future. For that reason, we will now identify your unique habits and determine which ones lead you away from creating your soul mate. Then you'll have the opportunity to create new ones that support your goal.

Identify Your Current Dating Habits

First you need to become aware of the habits you're currently and most frequently using while dating.

Here's a list of a few common dating habits:

Playing hard to get

Bragging about your accomplishments to make a good impression

Going out on a date three or four times then breaking up

Waiting to call until two days after the date rather than when you truly want to

Checking with a friend to get the "coast is clear" signal that she had a good time before you call her back

Refraining from letting him know you like him

Not dating because you're "too busy"

Interviewing people on the first date

Getting physically intimate and then beating yourself up the next day

Spending all your time e-mailing potential dates rather than actually meeting them

Pouring your heart out on the first date and then retreating

Talking too much about yourself and very rarely listening to your date

"Telling" your date how interested you are in him or her (flattery, sweet talking)

To be honest, my own dating habits were pretty counterproductive. For example, I'd date a girl for only a few months or less and then end the relationship before we got to know each other well. I never had a real reason for breaking it off, just that I wanted to leave her before she left me. After I did a little soul searching, it was pretty obvious where I created this habit. My mother passed away when I was 14 years old, and deep down I was afraid of being left again. Are fears such as these affecting you?

Honesty Pays Off

Laura dated guys just to have someone to do things with—go out for dinner, theater, walks in the park. She knew she didn't want children but kept that from them as long as possible. Whenever the conversation would turn to marriage and kids, she would sidestep the issue. When they'd finally find that out, they'd all leave. After a while, it got to be too painful to get attached and then lose relationship after relationship with wonderful guys. She resolved to be honest about having children up front, and now she's with a wonderful guy who shares her view.

Soul Mate Action Step 16: Take ten minutes to write down your dating habits. Use the examples above as food for thought. If nothing comes to mind, then try this: imagine that all the people you have dated all got together and talked about you. What patterns would they see? If you're still stuck, ask your friends. They'll know. Write down as many habits or "rules" as you can think of.

What did you notice? Was it uncomfortable? Did it feel good to tell one on yourself? In my seminars it's neat to see participants listen to each other's habits and laughingly identify their own. Whether you came up with a lot or a few, it's okay. The important thing is to raise your awareness of your automatic behaviors.

Without this awareness you'll most likely continue with the same patterns yielding the same old results. Are they aligned with who you are today and what you're committed to? Probably not, since you're still searching for your soul mate.

How Can I Shift My Limiting Dating Habits?

In identifying your current dating habits and how they limit you, you've probably naturally begun to design new, better ones for yourself. The key to creating new dating habits is to first uncover the subconscious beliefs that are holding the old ones in place. Often the most seemingly irrational behaviors make complete sense if you find the beliefs driving them. In the example I shared above, I would stop dating someone after only a few months for no real reason. However, given my hidden belief of "they'll leave me," it made sense for me to avoid the pain and break off the relationship first.

Bill's Breakthrough

Bill dated Rachel two or three times, and on the third date, Rachel asked him to go to a dance a month in the future. At first Bill felt uncomfortable, thinking, "If she's going to ask me on a date this soon and that far in advance then there must be something wrong with her." Bill waited to respond. Then he finally caught himself.

He realized that this was Rachel's way of showing that she liked him. Bill let his "dating guard" down and shifted his behavior. He said he'd go to the dance with her. Five months later, they were engaged. Bill took it one step at a time instead of jumping to conclusions.

To find your beliefs, listen to what you tell yourself to justify your dating habits. What do you say when you are about to take one of those actions on your list? In the example above, Bill's belief was "If she asks me out so soon and so far in advance of an event, there's something wrong with her." If he had acted consistently with that belief he might easily have found some reason to break it off then and there. His new dating habit was to "take it one step at a time instead of jumping to conclusions."

Here are some other examples of new dating habits you may want to adopt:

Communicate clearly and authentically

Date for quality not quantity

Trust the other person, or your instincts

Go to a wedding on the first date

Cook a fabulous dinner

Call first—before he or she does

Listen

Ask questions about his interests

Be confident

Give her the benefit of the doubt

Take your time before jumping in too deep, or...

Jump in instead of waiting for a certain amount of time to pass

Assume responsibility for how the dating relationship goes

Allow a good friendship to go farther

Mary's No-Brainer

Mary is an attractive woman who always dated "interesting" guys who were slightly aloof. She continually chased them and tried to make them fit into what she really wanted in a relationship. Meanwhile, other men would ask her out, and she would refuse. Why? In the back of her mind, Mary told herself "There's something wrong with guys who are too eager." Once she noticed this belief and the behavior that accompanied it, she decided to try a new tack: pay attention to the guys who are interested and allow them to come to her.

Not long after, she agreed to go on a date with a guy who had repeatedly asked her out before. To her surprise, she had the "date of her life." She was finally with someone who wasn't aloof and was genuinely delighted to be with her! Six months later he asked her to marry him. Mary is with her soul mate today.

Soul Mate Action Step 17: Now it's time for you to define and create your new dating habits. Using your list from *Action Step 16*, mark all of your dating habits or rules that you really want to change. For each of them, first identify the belief behind the habit. What is the excuse or justification you have for doing this? Write down whatever pops into your head. Then, create a new habit or rule. Take as long as you need to write down the new dating habits you want to cultivate now.

What hidden beliefs did you uncover? What new habits did you create? How do those habits feel? If you adopt these habits, what difference will it make in your future? Good work.

Bonus Action Step 1: Here's some bonus work. Write down exactly how you would act if you were about to meet your soul mate right now. What would make him or her proud of you? Start being that way right now. For example, you might behave like an elegant, classy woman or a dashing, debonair man. Act as if your soul mate depends on it. He or she does!

Bonus Action Step 2: Look at your relationship list from *Action Step 13* and compare this with your list of dating habits from *Action Step 16*. Do you see how you used any of your limiting dating habits in any of these relationships? (Hint: You probably do.) Since you're skilled now with having closure conversations with the people in your life, call someone from your list, and share with him or her what you've found out about your dating habits and limiting beliefs and what impact you think these had on your relationship. More than likely, this will be an enlightening experience for the other person too!

In many cases, actions really do speak louder than words. To attract your soul mate you must display those behaviors that will get you there. Congratulations on doing what's necessary to make that happen! The hard part is over. In the next chapter, you'll see how it all comes together.

Measuring Your Progress

16. I identified my limiting dating habits. Yes / No
17. I created new dating habits. Yes / No

Energy Meter – (circle your response)

5. I did all of my Soul Mate Action Steps passionately and put more effort into this than I've ever put into a creative project. I'm elated, exhausted, and my heart feels good.

4. I did all of my Soul Mate Action Steps passionately and put in extra effort. I went beyond my comfort zone.

3. I did all of my Soul Mate Action Steps to my highest ability.

2. I did some of my Soul Mate Action Steps.

1. I read the chapter.

Soul Mate Affirmations

• Each date brings my soul mate closer to me.

• My mind is clear.

• I am available in a new way.

Chapter 7

Tying It All Together

Think of all the work you've done over the course of the first six chapters: You committed to your Alive Line, you cleared out your physical space, you brought appreciation and closure to your relationships, and you looked at your dating habits and created new ones. In Chapter 8, we'll begin the creation process, but before we do allow me to share the story of how I met my soul mate, Thea. I've included the headings below to let you know how the parts of my story are tied to the work you're doing using this book.

I first heard the term *soul mate* in 1995 when I was playing pool with my friend Lisa at a bar next to our real estate office. We were taking a short rest from our daily activities of writing contracts and serving our customers. In response to a relationship question, Lisa bent over for a shot and said, "Maybe you're looking for your soul mate, Frank." I was hooked by the very first thought of it, even though I had no idea what a soul mate was. It seemed mysterious. She explained that it was someone whose compatibility matches you "to a T," and you end up spending your lives together in harmony, fulfilling your higher selves together. We had both been exploring the area of dating, and I always trusted Lisa's opinion because she had more experience with long-term relationships than I had. Despite my lack of experience, finding a soul mate seemed attainable to me. I don't know why, but it did.

From that moment, just knowing that my soul mate existed kept me on my quest, and, after four years of searching, I found my soul mate, Thea. What I didn't know was how I was actually creating her and attracting her to me with my thoughts and actions.

My Alive Line

In 1999, I entered a six-month-long personal development course. As a part of the course, I had the option of choosing an area of life in which I wanted to have a breakthrough. I chose several things: to increase my leadership skills, expand my songwriting and acting skills, increase my real estate business, and, last but not least, find my soul mate. I signed a commitment contract with myself like you did at the beginning of this book.

The course began with a lot of excitement and momentum. I also felt some fear and hesitancy. After all, it was an adventure into the unknown for me, an adventure I had not been willing to take before.

All 65 people in the course had tackled big goals, such as creating new jobs, leadership roles, marriages, careers, having children, and other such goals. Similarly, I was at work on the goals I had defined for myself. Once I learned how to open up to my classmates and welcome their contributions, my hidden obstacles and limitations began to quickly disappear.

Before the course, I was somewhat shy and scared to sing in public. Soon I was writing better songs, playing in a band, performing, and recording. Before I knew it, I was playing in front of 200 people at private parties. I had accomplished almost everything I said I would, except for finding my soul mate. I only had four weeks left in the course, and I knew that if I wanted to find her, I had to keep my word to myself.

Closure and Appreciation

The next four weeks were the most difficult but productive days of the course. I was afraid, confronted, and I feared it would not happen.

One day I stopped by my sister's apartment to pick up my brother. It was raining hard, and I ran from the car to her building and up the stairs to the sixth floor. When I entered, she asked me to remove my shoes. I said, "I will—just let me relax a minute." Meanwhile I walked over to her couch with my soaking shoes and sat down. She began to whine at me for not removing my shoes.

"Stop yelling. I will," I replied, and before you knew it an argument broke out.

From my perspective, I thought that what she had requested was a minor issue compared to my running all the way up the steps, and I couldn't figure out why she was being so nit-picky. "I'm a grown man. How can this be happening?" I thought.

The next day, I called a friend from my class and explained the situation. "Frank, how dare you not respect a woman's things," she exclaimed! I pulled the phone away from my ear because she was so right on. "Ouch. You are so right. Bingo," I conceded. At that moment, my entire life with my sister flashed before me. I had not been respecting women's things, especially my sister's things, for an entire lifetime.

My sister's request from the previous day didn't seem so unreasonable. I was acting like a child, and, rightfully so, she was treating me like one. I spent the next day apologizing for a lifelong trail of tiny disasters with my sister. She accepted my apology, and I listened to her and acknowledged her for having been so patient with me. All was forgiven, and a big source of resentment in our relationship was complete. Today, we have a much better relationship.

My Dating Habits

My next "aha" regarding women came shortly thereafter. I had been dating a girl for a short time. She was sick one night, and I had the bright idea to cheer her up by bringing a bunch of mutual friends over to her place as a surprise. I rang the doorbell at 11:30 pm, and she let me in thinking I was alone. I came in and asked how she was doing and then surprised her with the entourage coming in behind me.

She was furious! I couldn't believe it. I had good intentions; why was she so upset? Later, I realized that I had been completely inconsiderate, ignoring what she might have wanted for the sake of what

I thought was a good idea. The next day in an honest discussion, I apologized, and she forgave me.

Looking back, I know now that taking responsibility for my own limiting dating habits and cleaning up my relationships helped me lay a new foundation for attracting my soul mate. Without doing this critical work, there would have been no way for her to appear. Though it was emotionally draining, in hindsight, it was a miracle: I was free.

Down to the last three weeks of training, and I still hadn't.... I was soon dating another girl. I had gone out with her a few times, but knew she was not the one for me. We were at my home kissing on the couch, and suddenly it came to me.

I realized that time and time again, I'd used women for physical affection. I sought out women so I could feel wanted physically. This was a habit I had clung to for years, and once I saw the pattern I realized I had to let it go. Something inside me just said it wasn't consistent with my promise to have my soul mate. I openly admitted to my date that I couldn't do this anymore. "I have a confession to make. I am committed to finding my soul mate, and you, unfortunately, are not her. I'm sorry for leading you on. The next girl I kiss will be my soul mate, and I have three weeks to find her."

Surprisingly, she was genuinely happy and excited for me. We talked awhile, and she left. Frankly, I couldn't believe I'd had the courage to do it. I didn't stop there. I had a date set up for the next night with another girl. I called her and embarrassingly admitted my intentions. "I'm sorry, but I have to admit that I only wanted to make out with you. Don't take this the wrong way, but you're not the one, and I can't go through with this. I like you as a person, but I'm committed to finding my soul mate." She was floored. Then she said, "I'm not up to that either. You're so sweet." She was fine, and when we hung up, both of us felt good.

Getting Specific

The next day, I began making a list of the qualities I really wanted in my soul mate. I really got specific. I found myself asking for things I couldn't even believe I was asking for, like for her to be a great cook and an intellectual. I walked around the shopping mall thinking about what I wanted. I met my sister there and went over the list. She helped me refine it. I had no idea why I was doing it this way. I really didn't have faith in lists or that anyone would take mine seriously. I just went with it. I kept refining it that whole week.

Relaxing and Allowing

Two weeks left. The 65 of us from the course were at a party anticipating our course completion. We were all having great conversations, reveling in what we'd accomplished. Some had created new jobs or new relationships, others had reconnected with family members or gotten raises.

As the evening drew to a close, I got more and more frustrated. Everyone else had achieved such amazing things, yet I was still "looking" for my soul mate. I was perpetually looking. I hated it! Was it my destiny to always have that driving feeling of being the seeker? Why couldn't she come to me, I wondered? I turned to one of my friends and shared my frustration. I asked her, "What else can I do?" She looked at me and simply said, "Just stop looking." This was a novel idea and seemed impossible. How do you stop looking? I had no idea how to find her other than by looking. The next week, I explored this way of living.

One week and counting. I needed a break. I was sitting at an open house on a cold and rainy Sunday in March, and I needed to clear my head. I called a friend who was a flight attendant, and she was kind enough to let me use one of her tickets to fly standby to Miami. The very next night I was sitting on a park bench along Ocean Avenue watching people go by. I was totally unsettled. "Why am I here?" I asked myself. I got up and walked away from the crowd, across the beach to the ocean. I paced on the beach, watching the people and lovers go by. Finally, I'd had it. I mustered up the courage and began talking to God, right there in front of everyone.

"God, honestly—I've been a good person up to now. I've asked for the right woman to come into my life, and you haven't sent her...." I was overwhelmed with emotion, and by the end of my 15- or 20-minute conversation, I threw the book at God. I asked for my soul mate with all my heart, everything I had. I gave it my all. There was a point at which words made no difference; it was pure and utter emotional expression that drove my point home.

I specifically remember feeling like my words were coming from a source outside of me, just above my head, and straight through my heart. I had placed my final order. There was nothing to say or do—I simply had to let go and let God take over. I was no longer looking. I walked away from the ocean back toward the boardwalk with a feeling of peace and clarity. The next day, I took an evening flight home.

Synchronicity at Play

On the plane, I noticed some interesting synchronistic events. I sat next to a woman who asked me if I'd grown closer to God. Just out of the blue. I was blown away. For the nearly three-hour flight we talked about God and where I was with him or her or it. When I arrived home, I opened the closet and my copy of Neale Donald Walsch's *Conversations with God* tape fell out and hit my shoe. The phone rang moments later. It was my friend and priest, Father Don, reminding me of our lunch date the next day at noon. Amazing. It was as if God or the Universe was giving me little signs to let me know that he'd heard me!

March 27, 2000. The last day of the course. I was supposed to be tying up any and all loose ends from the preceding six months. I was feeling light and free to be. Every conversation I had was really heartfelt and fun. At about 7:15 pm, I found myself sitting across from a brown-haired, petite woman. I had seen her before and knew she was a participant in another course in the same organization.

Coincidentally, I had popped in on another course months ago and heard her say to her group that she'd had a breakthrough regarding men. I remembered it vividly. Before, when I'd tried to introduce myself to her, she'd blown me off. However, this time felt different. We spoke briefly. She was just beginning the same course I was finishing. We had a lot in common. She was interesting to talk to, and I thought it would be nice to get to know her better. At about 8 pm, I asked her if she wanted to go out for a drink or dinner later. I really had no romantic intentions. I was not looking, and I really don't even know why I asked. She accepted, but when 9 pm rolled around she was tired and asked to reschedule. She gave me her number, and I promised to call.

Many days later, I called and asked her out. She seemed startled that I'd called. She'd forgotten that I was going to call, and, truthfully, I'd even forgotten why I was calling, other than because I said I would. I cared a lot about keeping my promises, so I called. We set another date, and I met her after class. We discussed where to go. I remember so distinctly standing next to her and looking into her brown eyes. She was the perfect height for me. We agreed on a place and we took separate cars there. We found out later that it didn't dawn on either of us until the drive there that this was actually a "date!"

New Habits Pay Off

At the wine bar, I really listened to her when she talked. I just sat there cool and calm. I found that I liked what I heard, and she was smart. I wanted to get to know her more and more. She was elegant, refined, and a natural leader. I thought, "After all, I just finished a leadership course, and now she's starting it too. Why wouldn't I attract someone like her?" I understood her at a level I'd never understood anyone in my life. I had always wanted to be with a woman like this, and she'd always eluded me. Over the course of the evening, I shared a little bit of myself, but didn't have much to say. I just wanted to be with her and her essence.

I broke all the rules I'd previously set for myself. Within an hour, we were kissing on the couch in the wine bar and drinking a glass of wine in front of a fire. Somehow I knew that I'd found my soul mate, and I was going to do everything possible to keep her. I trusted myself and that God or the Universe had responded quickly. Most importantly, I was enlightened by the fact that things occur quickly when I ask, and all I need to do is be aware enough to notice them when they come. I was not going to allow anything to get in my way this time, not even myself.

It All Makes Sense

Looking back, I realized that finding my soul mate consisted of no more than resolving a series of unresolved issues. Once I shifted and resolved those issues, my soul mate came to me. In going backward, I'd moved forward. Not surprisingly, I later found out that she had been doing the same thing. Before we met, she had committed to shifting her limiting behaviors and beliefs with men, and had done some of the same things I had done in her own quest to find "the one." We were on two paths that had come together perfectly at the right time and in the right place. Six months later I asked her to marry me, and a year later she became my wife.

Looking back, I've come to the realization that despite the cynicism around dating in our culture today, underneath it all, men and women just want to find "the one." Despite our differences or which planet we're from, men and women both expect to love another and to be loved.

Of course, your journey won't look just like mine because you are unique. However, my hope is that you can use the wisdom I gathered along the way to meeting my wife to find your soul mate as quickly and easily, without all of the inauthentic game-playing that plagues the singles scene today. Hopefully, in the preceding chapter and in those that follow, I've added a few more tools to your tool chest than I initially had in mine. You have an edge now. A game. The remainder of this book will help you bring your soul mate into existence.

Soul Mate Action Step 18: Write a letter from the future as if you've found your soul mate already. You could address it to yourself, to God, to a family member, or to a friend. Share your delight and happiness, and how your soul mate is exactly whom you were hoping for. Describe your soul mate in detail. Acknowledge yourself for the work you did to attract him or her.

In the first six chapters, you looked at your past and brought closure to anything outstanding. Now that you have cleared the obstacles from your past out of the way, it's possible to align your thoughts and emotions with your future. Clearing is over. Now it's time to create.

In the next three chapters, you will design the structures, beliefs, and attitudes that will support you in creating your soul mate.

Measuring Your Progress

18. I wrote my letter from the future. Yes / No

Energy Meter – (circle your response)

5. I did all of my Soul Mate Action Steps passionately and put more effort into this than I've ever put into a creative project. I'm elated, exhausted, and my heart feels good.

4. I did all of my Soul Mate Action Steps passionately and put in extra effort. I went beyond my comfort zone.

3. I did all of my Soul Mate Action Steps to my highest ability.

2. I did some of my Soul Mate Action Steps.

1. I read the chapter.

Soul Mate Affirmations

- It's all coming together now.
- My soul mate is on the way.
- My hard work is paying off.

Chapter 8

Ready, Aim...Fire!

Did you know that 30 percent of a plane's fuel is used during takeoff? Up to this point you've just invested a lot of energy in preparation. Now it's time to lift off. It may seem like everything that's happened to you in your lifetime up to this point is one big accident. Sometimes you've gotten what you've wanted out of life and sometimes you haven't, but the whole thing is without rhyme or reason.

What if I told you that the Universe around you has been answering your every request, consistently delivering what you desire every single time? It has been and still is! It's called the Law of Attraction, and it's always operating—24 hours a day, 7 days a week. Then, you ask, why does it look like you're not getting what you want? The trick is knowing what message you're sending.

In this chapter, you'll learn the steps of the Law of Attraction and how to apply them to the task at hand. You'll learn how to attract more of what you want and less of what you don't want in your love life. As you master this simple process and hone your innate intuitive skills, you'll be able to deliberately create your soul mate with precise focus.

What Are Positive and Negative Vibrations?

"The best and most beautiful things in the world cannot be seen or even touched. They must be felt with the heart."
— *Helen Keller*

All thought is first generated from a feeling. Feelings give off energy. Energy is measured by scientists to give off a vibration. We judge our vibration basically in two ways: positive and negative. Whether it feels good or it doesn't. That's it. We think there are more variations, but all feelings boil down to these two. For instance, when we think of anger or sadness or resentment, it's all negative. Or when we think of happiness, joy, or exuberance, we call it positive. You can test it by whether it feels good. The Law of Attraction makes the world respond to how you feel. The results you get are a function of your mindset and emotions. That's part of the reason we went to such lengths in the earlier chapters to identify and eliminate sources of negativity in your relationships and environment, and to replace them with sources of positive energy.

What Is the Law of Attraction?

The Law of Attraction says "that which is likened to is drawn"—or more simply put, "like attracts like." It's all about where you put your attention. When you are focused on what you want, you are attracting what you want. When you are focused on what you don't want, you are attracting what you do not want. What you get is a function of what you are attracting, and what you are attracting is a function of where your thoughts are focused.

That's it. The Law of Attraction is actually quite simple and only takes practice to master; however, many of us have a tendency to make things more difficult than they need to be. When you get the hang of it with your soul mate, you'll be able to attract a lot more great things in other areas of your life too. Let's attract your soul mate first.

I had heard of the Law of Attraction but never knew that there were steps to learn or people who could teach them. Then I stumbled upon a free tele-class with Michael Losier, author of *The Law of Attraction*. In this conversation, he went over the steps, and, within one call, I was already beginning to apply them.

Wonderful things began to show up. I was about to purchase a home in Chicago. It was an incredibly difficult transaction that I kept feeling negative about, and yet I kept going through with it. On that first call Michael asked me a simple question: Is the general feeling positive or negative? I replied "negative." "Then why are you buying it?" he asked. Good question. The next day, the deal fell apart, and ever since I've only been working on things that I feel good about! If it feels good, it is.

A month after that conference call, I was ready for the next level. That's when I found my Law of Attraction coach, Dory Willer. She coached me for six months on how to utilize the Law of Attraction in my life. As I learned more and more, I realized the ways in which I had unwittingly used the Law of Attraction in finding my soul mate, three years earlier. Dory's extraordinary coaching is what gave me the courage to write this book.

(Michael Losier's book can be found at *www.lawofattractionbook. com*. It condenses the many years of teachings of the Law of Attraction by Abraham-Hicks (*www.abraham-hicks.com*.) More information on Dory Willer can be found at her website, *www.beaconquest.com*. A good, not-for-profit source of various Law of Attraction resources is *www.lawsofattraction.com*.)

The Formula for Success

The first step is to notice your "don't wants." This should be easy. We spend most of our time, it seems, focusing on what we don't want or don't like in a potential mate. These are things that you don't want and yet keep getting. Have you ever heard yourself say, "I'll never date anyone like that again"? Well, if you keep speaking that, the Law of Attraction says you will! For instance, your last boyfriend cheated on you. This was the last thing you wanted, and yet you ended up attracting it in the current relationship too.

Unfortunately, your "don't wants" are powerful subconscious thoughts and vibrations. Our goal is to shift your focus away from them after you gather the value they have for you.

The second step is to identify your "wants." Your "wants" are… well…what you really do want (not just "well it would be nice if…"), like a soul mate who is affectionate, loving, and responsible. You may think this is the easy part, but don't be surprised if it's challenging.

For some of us, focusing on the glass as half empty has become quite a habit. So what do you want?

The third step is to use your "wants" as a jumping off point toward what would really delight you. What would knock your socks off? This is where you really begin to tap into feelings of excitement and passion. Since your emotions are creating what you get, feeling good is critical to your success!

Some of your answers to this question will be in your list of "wants." (Why aren't all of them? Some of your wants are so closely related to the corresponding "don't wants" that they quickly "re-present" the negativity associated with them.) Sometimes this question will cause a whole new set of delightful qualities to come to you. Perfect. Your list of delights is purely positive and aligned with who you truly are and what you truly desire. Like sun through a magnifying glass, it focuses your positive energy and attention on what you really desire until it shows up. It's a deceptively simple process, yet unless you have a clear focus on what really makes you happy, you're like a loose cannon attracting a grab bag of both what you do and don't want, all the while wondering why you're getting what you're getting.

The fourth step is to raise your vibration or energy. How? Simply by focusing more and more on what you desire. With practice, you'll be able to notice an actual shift in your energy. It may occur for you as a feeling of well-being or happiness or increased physical energy. Have you ever noticed that things seem to go your way more when you're getting ready to go on vacation? It's due to the wonderful energy that your anticipation creates. It amps up your vibe. This is the reason that I suggested earlier that you schedule a vacation around your Alive Line.

Soul Mate Action Step 19: This exercise is critical in creating your soul mate. If you do only one exercise in this entire book, this should be the one. The four steps above are simple rules and tools; now let's apply them. On a sheet of paper, begin by making a list of your "don't wants" in a column on the right side of a page. In other words, the things you've been getting each time you date someone that you don't want. Do this now.

Then, for each of those "don't wants" ask yourself, "What **do** I want?" and create a list of your do wants on the left side. If what you don't want is someone who's angry, then you might write down "peaceful." Do this now.

Once you have the two sides complete, look at your list and ask yourself, "Now, what would really delight me?" Again, you may see some of the attributes that delight you on the "do want" list, but not all. Mark all of the "do wants" that delight you, and list them on a separate sheet of paper. Add anything that's missing—anything! What would really delight you?

Don't be surprised when you get *exactly* what you asked for. I do mean exactly, so be specific. For instance, if you were creating your ideal car and wrote down "I want a blue car," then you could end up with a blue car but one with only three wheels.

What you'll produce is your Soul Mate Resume. It may look something like Diane's on the following page. Do this now.

Sample Soul Mate Resume - *Diane's list*

Clarity via Contrast

Clarity (What I prefer/Like/Do want)	Contrast (What I have experienced/Don't want)
Someone who: 1. Is committed to growth and development 2. Has energy and intelligence 3. Is kind and has a sense of humor 4. Likes to travel and is artistic 5. Really likes and loves me 6. Loves his job and is joyful 7. Is peaceful, inspirational, and a leader 8. Wants children and loves family 9. Has facility and is great with money 10. Is romantic, sexy, good in bed, and attractive 11. We can both do anything we want together 12. Has great taste in clothing 13. Is spiritual and committed to bringing his higher side to the relationship 14. Is sensitive to my feelings 15. Is health-conscious	Someone who: 1. Is not willing to grow mentally and spiritually 2. Lacks energy and smarts 3. Is cranky 4. Is a homebody 5. Is ambivalent about how he feels about me 6. Resists his job and resists life 7. Yells 8. Doesn't want kids 9. Has money problems 10. Is sexually boring and unattractive 11. Only wants to do what he wants 12. Is not a good dresser 13. Is not spiritual 14. Is insensitive 15. Will let his physical health deteriorate

www.BeaconQuest.com

What would delight me?

Someone who:
1. Is passionately in love with me
2. Is smart and has a great sense of humor
3. Is a successful executive in a high-profile company
4. Loves his job and is respected by his colleagues
5. I can talk to about anything
6. Is sexy, generous, and good in bed
7. Will treat me like a princess!
8. Will explore fun new places with me: Amazon, Paris, or London, etc.
9. Has facility and is great with money, makes it, and can help me make it or make more
10. Surprises me with wonderful, considerate gifts
11. Has great taste in clothing and likes to shop
12. Appreciates romantic literature
13. Is a loving family member
14. Likes sports and funny movies but also enjoys documentaries and intellectual pursuits

©Copyright 1998 Beacon Quest Coaching   www.BeaconQuest.com

Remember, you'll get a mixture of the whole thing (including the "don't wants") unless your focus on "wants" and desires is greater than your focus on the "don't wants." The ultimate test: *If it feels good, it is*, so when you're not sure where your focus is, check your vibe!

Soul Mate Action Step 20: Create affirmations from your Soul Mate Resume list. Make sure to state them in the present tense as if you've already met your soul mate. Here are some examples:

My soul mate is peaceful, funny, inspirational, and a handsome leader.

My soul mate is a healer, abundant, creative, and sensitive.

My soul mate is wise, romantic, and an explorer of life.

Each day, choose one affirmation and write it ten times.

Ask and You Shall Receive

The next step is asking for it. Who do you ask? Ask God, Allah, Buddha, the Universe, your higher self, or the higher powers that be. Some people find it works to pretend that the Universe has an incredibly effective and totally reliable personal assistant assigned just for them, and pass the assignment along to them. Remember when I described how in Miami I asked God for my soul mate? Whatever the higher source is that you believe in, He/she/it/they will respond. In the form of the Law of Attraction, they always do, and now you're wiser and more accurate about what you're asking for.

When you ask, use your emotions. They'll get faster results than using your head. Our head worries about getting it right, while our heart just gets it out there. When I stood at the water's edge in Miami and "threw the book at" God, I was very emotional. I couldn't put my desire and longing into the right words but my emotions were 100 percent authentic. I got exactly whom I asked for.

"One minute of what goes on in terms of consciousness in your body could not be expressed in words in an entire lifetime."
— Abraham-Hicks

Allowing

The final step is allowing what you've asked for to happen. What is allowing? To put it simply, it's waiting for your order to come. It's been ordered. Forget about it. Stop looking. Go have fun and wait patiently for it to come to you. Talk to friends. Carry on with your life. The less doubt, faith, and anxiety you have around what you're asking for, the faster it will come. If you continue focusing on it *not* being there, then that's what you'll get more of—it not being there.

Part of allowing is releasing your doubts about getting it. Our doubts about getting what we want are actually a subtle form of resistance. This resistance is like static in the channel that prevents your authentic desire from getting through. Sometimes, our doubts spring from past experiences. All of the times in the past when we didn't get what we wanted build up as cynicism and doubt that we ever will. For this reason, the work you did in Chapters 2–7 helped to clear you of doubt and resistance.

It may seem initially as if you continue to get what you don't want, even though you're maintaining a positive energy and focus on your delights. This may very well be the Universe continuing to deliver based on past desires. I call this the "universal time lag," like the distance and time it takes after ordering from the drive-thru at a fast food restaurant to get what you asked for from the window.

Don't lose heart or allow your focus to shift back to the doubt and despair of "I never get what I ask for." Just notice what you get that you don't want, add it to your list, and go back to focusing on what you do want. You can also review Chapters 4 and 5 (your physical space and relationships), and use them to eliminate any more doubt or negativity that is holding you back. Continue doing this when needed.

It's useful to look at your relationship to speaking and getting what you want in general. When something doesn't meet your expectations, do you let people know what you want? Sometimes we have a surprising resistance to actually letting people know what would make us happy.

Having It His Way

Ray loved it that his previous girlfriend, Mona, always took him out to eat on his birthday. His current girlfriend, Jennifer, didn't know that, and isn't the type to do that anyway. When Ray's last birthday rolled around, he got upset when Jennifer didn't take him out, and she had no clue why. Sensing his frustration and wanting to please him, Mona asked, "What's wrong?" Ray responded, "Oh, never mind," and missed an opportunity to let her know exactly what he wanted.

Like Ray, we often choose to be upset with the ones we love rather than simply letting them know what we want.

Soul Mate Action Step 21: Begin to notice your own relationship to letting people know what you want. Practice speaking and clarifying exactly what you want. Notice what happens. You may add to your list of affirmations, "I always get what I want!"

Your Wants Give You Freedom

"Once I got clear about what I wanted in my relationship, I saw that one thing I really wanted but wasn't getting was communication. Finally, I got up the nerve to ask the man I was dating if he could provide that. After some thought he honestly replied, "No." In that moment, I was set free. I suggested that we stop dating, to which he agreed. Not long after that, I met the man of my dreams, who is my soul mate and husband today."

— Tatiana

You Definitely Get What You Focus On

Align thoughts and emotions with what you want. What does that mean? How do you do it? For example, if you are worried about paying a bill, you won't have enough money to pay the bill. Shift your thoughts and begin focusing on how delighted you are at having the bill paid. It's that simple. The Law of Attraction responds to every vibration you're putting out there. If your predominant vibration is positive, you'll get it.

FACT: Did you know that you need to focus on a feeling or vibration for only 17 seconds to match that equal vibration in the Universe and have it sent to you in some way, shape, or form? It's true!

Creating Collages to Create Images

I think one of the most impactful, wise, and affordable tools you can use to assist this process is a collage. You can create a collage from anything—pictures from your favorite magazines, postcards, or objects. Not only does the act of collecting the pictures and items and putting them together focus your creative energies on your soul mate, you end up with a visual display that keeps your goal in front of your mind and helps intensify positive vibrations. If you hang it prominently in your office or home, every time you pass by you refocus your attention on what you want.

Soul Mate Action Step 22: Go through all the beautiful magazines you enjoy reading and cut out pictures that represent the qualities on your Soul Mate Resume. What will you do together? Where do you want to go on vacation? Create a display by pasting them onto a piece of heavy paper and hang it somewhere you'll see it every day on a regular basis. Move toward joy and pleasure—see it visually! Go toward the light of what you're creating.

In this chapter, we've covered the simplest—and what I believe are the best—tools you'll need to create and attract your soul mate. If you've done the work, you have a whole new awareness of what you want and how to get more of it. Remember, if you're not getting what you want, focus on what you desire, not the absence of it. That's the key.

You get what you focus on. It's your job to tweak and hone these skills until your soul mate shows up. Enlist your friends to help you—they may have great ideas or remind you of things you've forgotten. Share the excitement of your journey. Every vibe counts.

The good news is you don't have to totally buy into the Law of Attraction for it to work for you. If you do the work, you'll begin to see synchronistic results right away. And of course, the more you focus on those results the more you'll get! Next, we'll look at six different habits that will support you in the creation process.

Measuring Your Progress

19. I wrote my Soul Mate Resume. Yes / No

20. I wrote my desire affirmation statements. Yes / No

21. I began noticing my relationship to letting people know what I want. Yes / No

22. I made a collage. Yes / No

Energy Meter – (circle your response)

5. I did all of my Soul Mate Action Steps passionately and put more effort into this than I've ever put into a creative project. I'm elated, exhausted, and my heart feels good.

4. I did all of my Soul Mate Action Steps passionately and put in extra effort. I went beyond my comfort zone.

3. I did all of my Soul Mate Action Steps to my highest ability.

2. I did some of my Soul Mate Action Steps.

1. I read the chapter.

Soul Mate Affirmations

• I feel positive, and I attract positive people and things.

• I know what I want and I get it.

• I am attracting what I really desire.

Chapter 9

The Six Degrees of Preparation

How Do You Support Your New Mindset?

Before planting seeds, a farmer tills the soil and fertilizes. Now that you've planted the seed of your Soul Mate Resume, it helps to create a hospitable environment for your soul mate to grow. Following are six habits, which I call the Six Degrees of Preparation^{SM}, that will keep your soul mate soil fertile and abundant.

1st Degree of Preparation

Believe that you can do it. Have a mindset consistent with a successful outcome. Expect your soul mate, be confident, have faith, and trust that he or she will show up. If you expect someone to prove something to you, then you aren't actually aligned with having it happen. You are saying, "I'll wait and see." You can't wait for someone to prove to you that it's possible. The Universe doesn't deliver on "show me and then I'll do it." There's no risk in that. So, believe it's possible and prove it to yourself! As Napoleon Hill said, "He had nothing to start with except the capacity to know what he wanted and the determination to stand by that desire until he realized it."

If you're having trouble believing, then turn your desired beliefs into affirmation statements. These will help you stay focused on your desires. If you work with them consistently, writing them each morning or repeating them to yourself, you'll shift your internal belief system. Here are a few examples.

"I am attracting my soul mate with every positive action I take."

"I've scheduled my vacation, and more good things are occurring in my life."

"I honor myself first."

What are three affirmations or beliefs you can write for yourself? Give your personal list of wants and desires positive attention every day. Carry it in your wallet or purse. (A list of Soul Mate Affirmations is available on *www.CreateYourSoulMateNow.com*).

2nd Degree of Preparation

Keep your promises. After you set your Alive Line, it's important to keep your word to yourself and others in all areas of life. We say, "Talk is cheap"—only if we make it so!

As humans, we have a tendency to make and break promises without much thought. In order for anyone else—including the Universe— to take what you say seriously, **you** must have a powerful relationship to your word. By making and keeping promises, whether it's "I'll turn this project in on Friday by 3:00" or "I'm going to exercise on Tuesday," each time you speak a promise and keep it you're training the Universe that what comes out of your mouth becomes reality.

Treat your Alive Line as a promise, one that you intend to keep no matter what gets in your way. It may be a struggle or a challenge. You may want to turn back, stop, or give up. You may get hurt or frustrated and want to go back to your old habits. You might get sick and use that as an excuse to not continue. Don't turn back! You are too close now.

Here's another way to look at it. If you have ever tried to push a car that ran out of gas, you know that it takes a lot of effort to get it rolling initially. Once it's moving, however, it takes relatively little effort to keep it rolling. When you don't keep your word to yourself, it's like having to get the car rolling over and over again. It is much easier to keep the momentum going.

Want a little extra "oomph"? Need a little extra help keeping your word to yourself? Tell others. Share your Alive Line and your soul mate project with as many other people as you can. Let them know in person, or by phone, e-mail, or letter. Ask them to support you and hold you accountable. They'll keep you focused when you get distracted, remind you when you forget, and support you in your quest. This can be a glorious time for you—working under some pressure can keep things interesting. You never know—you may discover new creativity that you never knew you had.

3rd Degree of Preparation

Give up deserving it. If you're secretly thinking that you're not good enough to have the person in your Soul Mate Resume, you'll never attract him or her. Your soul mate is a gift to you from the Universe. It has nothing to do with whether you're worth it or not. You aren't! None of us are. So give up waiting to be good enough.

4th Degree of Preparation

Look for coincidences. I've mentioned synchronicity before. Now is the time to recognize it fully. Notice that the quality you were asking for showed up in that person. Think about how peaceful the person is when all you had in the past was a boyfriend or girlfriend who complained. When the man asks you out and wants to take you to your favorite restaurant, don't be surprised. You created it. Welcome it.

Create a daily synchronicity journal. This will enable you to appreciate all the good things that are occurring around you. The more you appreciate these occurrences, the more you'll allow better things into your life. Your consciousness has expanded, so honor it.

5th Degree of Preparation

Leave room for error. You're trying something new, and you're going to make mistakes. If you do, so what? Don't give up. Just keep going. There are going to be people who you may think are "the one," and yet it may not work out. Take the wisdom you gain from these experiences back to your Contrast/Clarity worksheet (Chapter 8). Review your "wants," "don't wants," and desires. Where can you be more specific? Each new experience contains new seeds of clarity about what you want.

"One of the most common causes of failure is the habit of quitting when one is overtaken by temporary defeat. Every person is guilty of this mistake at one time or another."
— *Napoleon Hill*

Watch out for the tendency to be critical of yourself when you do make mistakes. After all, this is all new to you. Did you expect to learn a system overnight and get it to your standards without some practice? It took me ten years of personal development and training and more than 20 years of personal experience to put this system in place. So forgive yourself. Cut yourself a little slack. Give yourself time to absorb what is percolating in your soul.

Beware the pitfall of trying to do this system perfectly. The Action Steps were designed to assist you along your journey. There is no "right" way to do them. You will drive yourself nuts trying. The main point is to do them, experience the process and result, and learn the lessons each one holds. You have your own path, and that path is right for you.

6th Degree of Preparation

Speak positively. As I mentioned above in connection to keeping your promises, your word is very important. For the same reason, keep your speech free of negativity—blaming, gossip, and being critical. From the perspective of the Law of Attraction, such conversation focuses your attention on what you don't like and creates negative energy. It's like a one-two punch, guaranteed to get you what you don't want.

Although it seems harmless and natural enough (of course your best friend wants to know how your date went), gossip is particularly dangerous and has a serious impact on a person's character, **yours**! Gossip is poison and an energy drain, and feeds the worst in us. Bottom line: Negative speech and gossip make us less attractive of what we want and less attractive, period.

A Dangerous Slip

Laura and Sandra were in a coffee shop. Sandra was talking about the new guy she's been dating, how they'd really hit it off, and how nice she thought he was. However, later on she found herself making fun of Ron's car—a 1991 Camaro. Fueling the fire, her friend chimed in, "What does that say about his personality? What kind of 31-year-old still drives a college car?" Not surprisingly, Sandra began to have other doubts about Ron as well. "Yeah, I guess it is kind of dorky." What they didn't know was that Ron's friend Chuck was standing right behind them. Moments later, Ron heard from Chuck an even less flattering version that what had been said. Upset, Ron never called Sandra again.

What do you do if you find yourself gossiping? First—stop. Second, if you're really bold and dedicated to clearing any negative energy you have around, clean it up with the person you spoke about. "Hey, Mary, I just wanted to let you know that I said something unkind about you to Joe. I just wanted to apologize." Sound crazy? Maybe, but do it once, and it will definitely nip the gossip bug right away. You may find that you start having much more interesting and positive conversations with your friends and family.

Soul Mate Action Step 23: Clean up any times you may have gossiped in the past.

In this chapter, you learned the Six Degrees of Preparation. Make these your new standards. Living by them will create fertile soil where your soul mate can grow. It may take you a little time to digest this material. But by setting the bar high for yourself, and by becoming masterful at these tenets, you will begin to yield higher results in life.

If you're thinking that it can't get any better than this—well, it's about to. Remember the objects you tossed back in Chapter 4? Now it's time to replace them with what your heart desires.

Measuring Your Progress

23. I've cleaned up gossip that I spread. Yes / No

Energy Meter – (circle your response)

5. I did all of my Soul Mate Action Steps passionately and put more effort into this than I've ever put into a creative project. I'm elated, exhausted, and my heart feels good.

4. I did all of my Soul Mate Action Steps passionately and put in extra effort. I went beyond my comfort zone.

3. I did all of my Soul Mate Action Steps to my highest ability.

2. I did some of my Soul Mate Action Steps.

1. I read the chapter.

Soul Mate Affirmations

- I always keep my word to others and myself.

- I believe in myself.

- I am prepared for my soul mate.

Chapter 10

Finishing Touches

This is the really fun part. Remember all those items that you cleaned out of your physical space? All those photos, furniture, compact discs, and clothing you let go of? It may have seemed tempting to immediately replace them with other things. However, without your new mindset, it was most important for you to wait. You could have replaced most of those items with similar ones that represent your unconscious mindsets or limiting beliefs, which would have been counterproductive.

Now we'll look at what you can put **into** your space to welcome your soul mate. Let's start with fresh new things in your environment. Your old objects kept you anchored in your past, and now you're upgrading in order to stay anchored in what you desire. (I recommend you refer to *Move Your Stuff, Change Your Life: How to Use Feng Shui to Get Love, Money, Respect, and Happiness* by Karen Rauch Carter.)

Start With Your Closet!

You may want to consider starting with your closet. What does your closet say about you? Does it support two people? Is it well designed? Is it inviting and warm? Is there an equal amount of space for both of you? Is it well organized and clear? Does it feel good to wake up and start your day by choosing what's available to you? Your closet is where you start every single day, so it's important that you like it. To start working on your closet, you might create a collage of the kinds of clothes you like or a picture of an organized closet from a great magazine and put it up so you can begin to organize and sort out your life that way.

Clothing is a reminder of who we are. "The clothes make the person." You make a choice about who you are each day through the clothes you choose to wear. You could say that your closet is where you store your identity.

Your clothing also plays an important role in attracting your soul mate. First, clothes are an outward way of telling people how you feel about yourself. Your clothes should fit well, be clean and neat and flattering to your figure, all of which communicates that you care about yourself and are proud of who you are. If you don't care, why should anyone else? Second, in terms of the Law of Attraction, clothing can be a powerful way of creating and maintaining a positive vibration all day. For this reason, too, it's important to notice how your clothes make you feel.

So when you search for new "attractive" clothing, first ask yourself how it feels. Your feelings, not your thoughts, are the most important measure or test as to whether a new piece of clothing serves you or not. Ask yourself: Does it give me energy or take it away? Does it offer me the style, fit, and comfort I want? Is it aligned with what I created in my Soul Mate Resume?

Those descriptive words and ideas belong in your clothing. As you build your wardrobe with items that add to your energy and liveliness, you'll be aligning your exterior with your interior and adding momentum to getting your soul mate. After I met my soul mate, guess where we coincidentally saw each other shopping one day? At our favorite clothing store!

Soul Mate Action Step 24: Buy yourself a new favorite piece of clothing using these principles.

Creating Soul Mate Space in Your Bedroom

Next go to your bedroom. Think about it—your bedroom is where you spend a **third** of your lifetime! What does your bedroom need that would invite romance? What about the other characteristics on your Soul Mate Resume? Romance, warmth, sex, conversation, relatedness?

First think *pairs.* Do you have two nightstands next to your bed? If not, get another one. The Universe responds to what you're putting out there, and if you have only one nightstand, then you're reinforcing the message that you're single. Fill your bedroom with items that match—matching candles, lamps, rugs, romantic items. This represents parity and equality in your relationship. Acquire the things you've always wanted, and those same qualities will show up in your soul mate. Your bedroom should be comfortable, like a nest. What have you been putting off buying for your bedroom? Your instincts at this point are pretty good. Go buy those things. Think about what it would represent and go for it. Add the qualities of the person you'd like to attract. If you like loyalty, then get a picture of a dog for your dresser.

How about your bed? Does it support two people? If you're still sleeping in a single bed, then you literally haven't created the space for your mate to show up. Are you still sleeping on a futon? Is your bed comfortable? Your bed represents the foundation of your future relationship. It also provides a stable platform for the work of your unconscious while it busily connects with the Universe to attract your soul mate.

Buy a grand bed that will last, and treasure it with your partner for a lifetime. The principles of feng shui, the Chinese art of objects and energy, are specific about beds: Avoid beds that rest directly on the floor (they don't allow energy to flow underneath them) and beds with no headboard (a headboard represents support, and you need support in your life). Don't place your bed with the head against a window, which leaves you vulnerable. It's best if your bed is arranged so that it faces the door of your room. If you can't afford a bed with a headboard, you can decorate the wall with artwork or a poster. Footboards, too, provide stability. For more on this, refer to *Move Your Stuff, Change Your Life....*

Soul Mate Action Step 25: What are the colors in your bedroom? Are they warm, bright colors or dark, lonely colors? Paint or decorate your bedroom with the colors of love: soft pinks or reds (the color of passion). (Yes, guys, I said pink. You bought pink power ties in the 1980s. You can have pink in your bedroom.) Lovers adore luxurious and clean linens. Again, this will boost your energy as well as be aligned with your quest to attract romance. Remember to make it smell good too.

Clear a space for romance by putting the television, computer, desk and exercise equipment in rooms other than your bedroom.

Your bedroom is the most important place to build your new relationship. Make it your sacred space. The more you raise the physical energy level of your environment, the more you'll raise your vibration to attract and keep what you want.

Guy Tips: Avoid "bachelor" art such as cars, centerfolds or sports figures.

Girl Tips: Avoid crowding your bed with stuffed animals, dolls and unnecessary pillows.

Soul Mate Action Step 26: Make a list of everything you'd love to have for your bedroom right now. Take only two minutes and write everything you can think of. Go! Now take action to acquire these items. Buy a new bed, nightstand, or pair of items to place in your bedroom.

Who do you need to call? What stores are you thinking of? What friend has an item that he or she is getting rid of? What do you need to do to get these items? Go do it.

Add Details to Other Rooms in Your Home

Let's look around your home. Does your bathroom have two towels? Then grab two towels and put them there. Is it clean? There's no bigger turnoff than a grimy bathroom. Honor yourself and your soul mate by keeping it clean. Do you have a couch with enough room to snuggle up with another person, or is there only one place to sit? Does your dining room table or kitchen table have only one chair and one place setting? Get two. Get the point?

Television Out, Soul Mate In

"I was searching for my soul mate and attended your seminar. Afterward, I noticed that I was still hanging on to a television that had come from my ex-fiancé, housed in an entertainment center built by an ex-boyfriend! After what I learned in the seminar, I realized that they both had to go. I bought a new, wonderful TV and then found the perfect entertainment cabinet to fit it—and believe it or not, it's a beautiful red color. Two weeks later, a friend set me up with Tyler. We're now in a committed soul mate relationship."

— Wanda

Pay close attention to what's at eye level in your space. I have a theory that whatever is going on in the present and where you're going in the future is at your eye level. What's directly on your walls at eye level? I remember hearing a story from a feng shui practitioner. She had a client who had pictures of single, lonely women on her walls. What did this bring her? You guessed it, life as a single, lonely woman. The woman began putting new images of what she wanted on her walls, and men began showing up for her. Choose images for your own walls that reinforce where you're headed instead of where you've been.

Soul Mate Action Step 27: Look at the other rooms of your home. Buy three more objects that resonate with who you are and who your soul mate is.

You have symbolically closed one door to allow another to open. Everything is constantly changing, and so are you. Your environment is a powerful way to reinforce what you're creating in your life and to maintain focus on what you desire. Align your physical space with your soul-mate-to-be and you'll draw that person to you even faster. You've done great work so far. We're almost through. Are you ready to wrap things up?

Measuring Your Progress

24. I bought a new favorite piece of clothing. Yes / No

25. I made a list of everything I'd love for my bedroom. Yes / No

26. I acquired a new bed or nightstand. Yes / No

27. I acquired items from my desire list. Yes / No

Energy Meter– (circle your response)

5. I did all of my Soul Mate Action Steps passionately and put more effort into this than I've ever put into a creative project. I'm elated, exhausted, and my heart feels good.

4. I did all of my Soul Mate Action Steps passionately and put in extra effort. I went beyond my comfort zone.

3. I did all of my Soul Mate Action Steps to my highest ability.

2. I did some of my Soul Mate Action Steps.

1. I read the chapter.

Soul Mate Affirmations

• I energize my home with possessions I love.

• My environment honors who I am.

• My home welcomes everyone.

Chapter 11

Following Your Heart

"Love is but the discovery of ourselves in others, and the delight in the recognition."

— Alexander Smith

Y ou've done some pretty extraordinary work during this process, so take some time to acknowledge yourself for it.

Many of you have already met your soul mate. Congratulations! Share your abundance with others and help them create their soul mate.

You may be with someone, and you know he or she is your soul mate, but your partner doesn't. That's okay. Give your partner time. Continue creating. My soul mate didn't know either. I kept creating. It wasn't until we were together for over a year and were already engaged for five months that she said those beautiful words to me, "You are my soul mate, Frank." In my mind, that's bigger than "I love you." That's a heartwarming, eternal kiss.

Some of you may still be creating and happy with the process. You've got time on your Alive Line. Keep up the good work.

Others of you, still committed, may be totally concerned, frustrated, or overwhelmed and don't know where you stand because your soul mate hasn't shown up yet. It's okay—you're in action, working on what's most critical for your success. Welcome your emotions, whatever they are, as a sign that you're engaged with the process. You have no idea—you might meet your soul mate in the next hour or day. Trust, and that trust will create a space for him or her to show up.

You may be out of the game completely. You decided that this is not for you. And that's okay too. You gave it the old college try. You're finished and complete with it.

Regardless of where you are, honor your path.

Currently, you have more than enough tools to finish the job and choose. If you've done the work, you'll feel confident and competent. You don't have anything to worry about. Recognize your soul mate by following your feelings. When you're around that person, you'll feel lighter, energized. Your soul will recognize your soul mate, and you'll feel it beating whenever he or she is near. You will feel no ambivalence.

If you're not sure, return to your Soul Mate Resume and see what's there. Trust yourself, and have fun. Creating your soul mate is a function of what *you* put into it, now and in all the years you will be with that person. So stick with it. If you need to recommit to your personal Alive Line, then do so. It's your life.

Tips for When You Get Stuck

One: Rearrange the objects in your environment. Whether you are stuck or not will be a natural sign of whether you are progressing and moving forward or regressing and moving backward. Guard your energy and keep it high.

Two: Use the people in your community for support, and if you know other people who are reading this book, form a group. Help each other do the Soul Mate Action Steps.

Three: Appreciate, appreciate, and appreciate! Allow the momentum to continue by affirming and appreciating what has been showing up that you're proud of—even little things, like you got reacquainted with a friend from long ago, your boss gave you more responsibility, or you took in a homeless puppy. Generate more good thoughts and feelings, and you'll radiate more of your positive energy.

When I Find My Soul Mate, Will Our Relationship Always Be Good?

Are you kidding? You may hate each other at times and feel incredible compassion for each other at other times. Extremes exist everywhere. Know that they will always be there.

Your soul mate relationship is always a mirror of who you are, reflecting back to you your traits and qualities. Sometimes they reflect the work that is not yet finished in you. This may challenge you. The degree to which you love yourself will determine your ability to love the other person. He or she is there to help you see your true self. Assist each other. Serve each other.

Let go of thinking that your soul mate will fulfill your every expectation. He or she won't. It's impossible. Don't focus on being together for better or worse, but for better or best!

You'll be incredibly surprised at what you create. Sure, there are aspects of my soul mate that I didn't anticipate—both good and bad. But the good far outweighs the bad. In my heart, I'm clear that she's the one.

Will I Ever Get It Right?

Probably not. It's a journey—the point is that you create it. Your soul mate doesn't have to be perfect—after all, you're not perfect, right? It's not about getting it right. There is no right way except your own. You can create as you go, and that creative process will continue long after you've met. Most people deal with their mate as if he's the final product. She's not; we're all in the making. The point is to have that wonderful companion on the journey to self-realization.

Our entire journey is about being present, not perfect.

"You've come to love not by finding the perfect person, but by seeing an imperfect person perfectly."

— Sam Keen

The Key to Keeping Your Soul Mate:
Express Gratitude Daily

Are you beginning to sense a theme here? Express gratitude for everything you love about your new soul mate—her thoughtfulness, his strength, her culinary abilities, his mechanical prowess, her financial wizardry, and his stunning good looks—and tell the world. The more grateful you are for that person and his or her extraordinary qualities, the more you're going to receive a similar energy back.

Go the Extra Mile

You set the date of your Alive Line a while ago. Don't turn back. Keep your promise to yourself, and it will be your fuel for eternity. If you keep your momentum going, it will carry you forward. Don't start and stop and start and stop. That journey will be slow and frustrating. Would you rather take the local bus to your soul mate or the express bus? The question is "How badly do you want it?" Do what it takes to create your soul mate. Don't hold back!

Everything in this book is designed to challenge you and push you to go beyond who you know yourself to be. I invite you to stretch your notion of yourself to being someone who is ready for the love of his or her life. Asking for your soul mate requires great emotional focus and power. You know what they say—watch out what you ask for, you just might get it.

> *"You know what happened to the boy who got everything he ever wanted, don't you? He lived happily ever after."*
> —*Willy Wonka*

Soul Mate Action Step 28: Go to the website *www.CreateYourSoulMateNow.com* and declare that you have found your soul mate. Then, if you like, e-mail me your story of how you found your soul mate (*frank@CreateYourSoulMateNow.com*).

Love, Frank

Measuring Your Progress

I completed this book with all my heart, soul, desire, and love.
Yes / No

Soul Mate Affirmations

- I found my soul mate.

- My soul mate is within my grasp.

- I follow my heart.

Afterword

You have been engaged and focused on your soul mate for an entire book, however long that may have been. The likelihood of you attracting your soul mate is very high. Remember, "You get what you focus on."

Once you have absorbed the soul mate process fully, give this book away. Keep it moving. It's important that someone else use this valuable information to create his or her soul mate too. You may even notice something magical as you give it away. The person who receives it may help you! And if you need to look at the book again, it will appear.

Share the breakthroughs you've had using this book with many people. The difference it made in your life could make a difference in theirs as well. We are all on this planet to heal, to be at peace, to cherish one another, to spread happiness, and to prosper.

Resources and Recommended Studies

Books:

Carter, Karen Rauch. *Move Your Stuff Change Your Life: How to Use Feng Shui to Get Love, Money, Respect, and Happiness.* New York: (FIRESIDE) Simon and Schuster 2000.

M. V. Hansen, and R. G. Allen. *The One Minute Millionaire: The Enlightened Way To Wealth.* New York: Harmony Books 2002.

Hill, Napoleon. *Think and Grow Rich* New York: Fawcett Books 1960.

Kingston, Karen. *Clear Your Clutter with Feng Shui.* New York: Broadway Books 1999.

Losier, Michael. *Law of Attraction Book.* Michael Losier 2003. *www.LawofAttractionBook.com*

Tapes:

Hicks, Jerry & Esther. *A New Beginning I & II.* San Antonio: Abraham-Hicks Publications 1988, 1991. *www.Abraham-Hicks.com*

Hyder, Carole J. *Wind and Water: Your Personal Feng Shui Journey.* California: The Crossing Press Freedom 1999.

Personal Growth and Training:

The Landmark Forum, Introduction to Leaders Program and Wisdom Course - Landmark Education World Headquarters - San Francisco, Ca *www.landmarkeducation.com*

The Mike Ferry Organization - Neural Linguistic Programming – Coach: Matthew Ferry, Newport Beach 2003. *matthew@mikeferry.com*

Beacon Quest Coaching - Dory Willer - Guiding Personal & Professional Potential *www.BeaconQuest.com*

The Second City Training Center – Pipers Alley Chicago *www.secondcity.com*

How to contact Frank Polancic
www.CreateYourSoulMateNow.com

A newly developed website, regularly updated, with soul mate stories, soul mate declarations, and details of Frank's courses, speaking engagements, and products.

Frank Polancic
P.O. Box 408017
Chicago, Il 60640-9998
www.frankpolancic.com
E-mail: *FrankPolancic@CreateYourSoulMateNow.com*

Where do you order Frank Polancic's products?

www.CreateYourSoulMateNow.com or call toll free (888) 551-1129

Workshops
"Why Wait? Create Your Soul Mate Now!"

Fun, engaging and powerful workshops designed to assist participants at creating a soul mate for their hearts desire.

Tele-seminars

Programs designed to keep you passionately creating after you leave the workshop or finish the book.

Professional Speaking Engagements

I speak about the topic of creating your soul mate to large groups or at private events.

Products

My other works include "Create Your Soul Mate Now!" affirmations compact disc, and affirmations.

Upcoming Products

Workbook, Journal, Audiotape, Audio Workshop, Board Game, E-zine, E-course, Soul Mate World Retreat

About the Author

Frank Polancic knows firsthand what it feels like to seek and find a soul mate. He used the techniques described here to meet and marry his wife, Thea. Frank is a successful businessman, sought-after speaker and the leading authority on creating soul mates. He has been extensively trained in traditional and non-traditional methods of personal transformation and achieving life goals. He combines these approaches in an innovative, powerful method for identifying and attracting your soul mate. You'll find his method an engaging, accessible, and fun approach to your most heartfelt quest.

WHY WAIT?
Create Your Soul Mate Now!

Order more copies of Frank Polancic's book

Why Wait? Create Your Soul Mate Now!

You can mail this order form to:
Frank Polancic
P.O. Box 408017
Chicago, IL 60640

Please enclose a check made out to *Jammytime*.

Order by Phone **(888) 551-1129** (have your credit card handy)
Order online at *www.CreateYourSoulMateNow.com*

Price is $19.95 per book (Illinois residents add $1.75 sales tax per book)

Shipping $3.85 *for first book (add $1.00 for each additional book)*
Outside USA please e-mail for shipping rates info@CreateYourSoulMateNow.com

Please send me _____ books

Name: _____

Mailing Address: _____

E-mail: _____

Phone #: _____ Fax #: _____

Payment:__VISA __ Mastercard __AMEX __ Discover (check one)

Card #: _____ Exp. Date: _____

Name on Card: _____

Signature: _____

Card Billing Address: _____

ORDER TOTAL:$ _____

Volume or Resellers e-mail *bulkorders@CreateYourSoulMateNow.com*